RETURN TO
H
HOD

G000023823

Hertfordshire
COUNTY COUNCIL
Library Service

Please return this book
on or before the last
date shown or ask for
It to be renewed.

L32

1 3 JAN 1993

0 2 MAR 1991   1 3 MAR 1993   2 5 OCT 1995

0 4 JUN 1991   3/4/93

09 OCT 1993

2 7 SEP 1991   2 8 MAR 1994   1 6 NOV 1998

1 1 NOV 1991   2 0 APR 1994

2 3 DEC 1992   1 0 JAN 1995

HERTFORDSHIRE LIBRARY SERVICE
WITHDRAWN FOR SALE
PRICE:

SMUGGLING

SMUGGLING

A History 1700–1970

DAVID PHILLIPSON

DAVID & CHARLES : NEWTON ABBOT

This book is not an official publication, so the Commissioners of Customs & Excise can accept no responsibility for its contents.

0 7153 6087 6

© David Phillipson 1973

All rights reserved. No part of this publication may be reproduced, stored in a retrieval system, or transmitted, in any form or by any means, electronic, mechanical, photocopying, recording or otherwise, without the prior permission of David & Charles (Holdings) Limited

HERTFORDSHIRE
COUNTY LIBRARY   21 176 7666

364.133

6144289

Set in 11/13pt Bembo
and printed in Great Britain
by Biddles Limited Guildford
for David & Charles (Holdings) Limited
South Devon House Newton Abbot Devon

To P.A.
Cutter commander
in the best tradition

Contents

	Preface	11
1	The Smugglers	13
2	The Revenue Cutters	32
3	Some Shortcomings	50
4	Smugglers' Devices	60
5	East and West	76
6	Blockaders and Coastguard	94
7	Encounters at Sea	113
8	Modern Smugglers	127
	Glossary	146
	Bibliography	149
	Acknowledgements	151
	Index	153

List of Illustrations

Customs Rate Book c 1790   18

Magistrates' Manual of 1722   20

The smuggler's grave   27

Robert Burns' survey book   29

Page from register kept by Burns' superior at Dumfries   30

William Arnold's residence at East Cowes   35

Model of Revenue cutter, c 1800   37

Sketch of Revenue cutter *Repulse*   42

HMRC *Valiant* at speed   42

Cutter commander's fan mail   53

Revenue cutter *Greyhound*   55

Matchlock musket   58

Sketch of method of hiding brandy kegs   61

Typical concealments in hull construction   70

Waterguard rummage crew at work   74

Hawkhurst gang breaking into Poole Custom House 79

Murder of Galley and Chater 83

Smugglers bringing goods up from the beach 92

A Riding Officer's arms 99

Revenue cutter *Viper* 102

Dragoons intercepting smugglers 105

Officers and crew of *Vigilant,* 1906 109

HM trawler *Esther* before conversion during the 1920s 111

Esther after conversion to become Revenue cutter *Vigilant* 111

Revenue cutter *Swan* engaged by French privateer 121

Steam Revenue cutter *Argus* 125

'Isles' class armed trawler *Benbechula* 129

A Waterguard officer hails an arriving yacht 133

A boarding party from HMRC *Venturous* 137

Cannabis concealed in cine-film tins 142

Cannabis resin slabs from Pakistani vessel 144

Container lorry from Kabul 145

Preface

This brief history of smuggling was prompted by my reading of a highly coloured and admittedly fictitious account—one of many such —which portrayed the old-time smugglers as gallant champions of the people, risking their lives and property to bring in a little untaxed comfort. Robin Hoods in seaboots, in fact. I was privileged during my service at various out-ports and creeks to leaf through original records of the eighteenth century. These were written in beautiful copperplate and recorded in an official, detached fashion many deeds hardly consistent with the romantic view: for instance, the severing by cutlass blade of the two hands of a Customs officer who was attempting to board a suspected vessel, and the prolonged torture and cold-blooded murder of a (wrongly) suspected informer. Such events had in contrast convinced me that the smuggler of yore was a bird of a very different feather. Further research has strengthened my conviction that smugglers (with honourable exceptions, notably among Westcountrymen) were as ripe a bunch of villanous, bloodthirsty and contemptible cut-throats as ever besmirched England's fair name.

I cannot do better than quote the words of a writer whose duties brought him into daily contact with these much romanticised 'free-traders'—Lieutenant R. Warneford, RN, appointed to the Coastguard in 1826:

> I am about to jot down a few rough adventures in the Preventive Service of this country which will present no fancy pictures of high souled, dashing smugglers, such as I have seen spouting heroics at minor theatres—rollicking gentlemen, who abound in all the first-rate virtues of generosity, daring, gallantry, and skill, slightly clouded, if at all, by an irresistible propensity for defrauding the revenue—more, it is usually made to appear, for the fun and dash of the thing, or to rig out amiable sweethearts or devoted wives with expensive nick-nacks, than for any liking for the, in the main, idle and skulking life of the professional smuggler. I never ran athwart any such gentry; but then it is right to state that my experience was confined to a couple of hundred miles or thereabouts of the southern coast of England, and those heroes, I fancy, are only to be found, if at all, in latitudes frequented by their relatives—the horse-marines.

My own view, exactly.

I

The Smugglers

It is impossible totally to prevent smuggling . . . all that the Legislature can do is to compromise with a crime which, whatever laws may be made to constitute it a high offence, the mind of man can never conceive as at all equalling in turpitude those acts which are breaches of clear, moral virtues.

Lord Holland, Parliamentary Debate, July 1805

Faversham Creek, on the north coast of Kent: the time is 4am; the date, 9 January 1969. A chill wind sighs over desolate mudflats, rattling the dry reeds. The night is moonless; dark clouds race low across the sky.

To the watchers on the shore, straining eyes and ears seaward, the wind carries a faint spluttering of an engine and the slap of water on a boat's bluff bows. Soon they pick out its black shape, squat hull and lofty wheelhouse, as it noses towards the shoreline.

A voice from the deck calls out, warning of shallows; the engine roars as the boat backs off into midstream in a froth of dark water. Again it approaches, fumbling for a landing. It turns away, thwarted, and lies still, stemming the beginning of the flood-tide with engine throbbing. A clanking of anchor chain, then silence.

The two men crouching in the reed-bed talk in low voices; one bends to a pocket radio and speaks into it. They resume their vigil.

Hours pass; a pale hint of dawn appears through the overcast. The watchers ease their cramped limbs. The man with the radio leans forward to peer beyond the fringe of reeds towards the broader water of the estuary. His companion sits slumped and motionless, but lifts his head as he hears the sound for which they are waiting: the deep growl of powerful motors at low throttle, borne fitfully on the freshening wind. Their quarry lies still and silent, unsuspecting.

The engine's note draws nearer and through the murk of the bleak mid-winter morning appears a grey silhouette, flared bows towering, water hissing down sleek sides. A cluster of figures stand on deck. One turns and calls to the bridge. At the same moment the two ashore rise from their nest in the reeds and stand erect, stiffly in their oilskins. They raise their arms above their heads, thumbs jabbing upwards, and receive an answering wave from the approaching craft.

A light flicks on in the wheelhouse of the moored vessel. A face appears, blurred, at the window. The door is flung open; a shout, and three men stumble on deck. They stand transfixed as they sight the looming outline of the Revenue cutter bearing down. A voice hails them, snatched on the blustering wind.

'Customs patrol. Stand by, we are coming aboard.'

The cutter edges alongside and two uniformed figures jump down to the boat's deck . . .

The foregoing is not a fanciful episode in a tale of smugglers versus Revenue men. It is a factual account of a contraband run, one of many intercepted on the coasts of the United Kingdom in recent years. This was a good haul—160,000 cigars—which, successfully landed and disposed of, would have entailed a loss to the Revenue of £12,000. The three men, together with an accomplice ashore, were tried at Kent Quarter Sessions on a charge of attempting to evade the duty on the cigars. They were convicted and sentenced to terms of imprisonment. The contraband was seized, together with the smugglers' boat.

An ironic twist to this story is that the boat involved began life as a Customs launch, served for many years in that capacity, and was eventually offered for sale when her useful working days were over. It seems likely that this shameful episode marks the close of her long career; at the time of writing she lies forlornly in a Kentish creek, awaiting the pleasure of HM Commissioners of Customs and Excise.

The Revenue cutter which made the capture is one of the latest in a long line. Little is known to the general public of these craft; seagoing yachtsmen encounter them occasionally, perhaps when they are 'spoken' on passage through coastal waters, or when the cutter pays a discreet visit to a yachting centre. But Revenue cutters, as we shall see, have played a major role in Britain's unceasing war against the smuggler over the centuries.

The United Kingdom, with a total of 6,000 miles of coastline and much of it in close proximity to the Continent of Europe, is obviously vulnerable to sea-borne smuggling. Its coasts have always been particularly tempting to the determined smuggler, with many good landing-places in spots remote from habitation. Some of these have recently been taken advantage of by the fraternity who carry human contraband in the shape of illegal immigrants; little is new under the sun where smuggling is concerned, and this particular form of it has given rise to concern many times in the past.

The heyday of smuggling in England was roughly the century and a half from 1700 to 1850. It had been a popular occupation for centuries before that period, but consisted rather in the illicit exportation of goods than in import smuggling as we know it today. From Tudor times and earlier the export of raw wool, England's staple product before the Industrial Revolution, was totally prohibited in order to encourage the home weaving industry which was struggling in competition with the Flemish and French. As a result English wool growers, denied foreign markets, were obliged to accept whatever price was offered by home manufacturers. In spite of the embargo, however, a large proportion of the national output found its way to France and the Netherlands, notably through the exertions of the notorious 'owlers' (see glossary) of Romney Marsh.

Smuggling activity over the years has naturally waxed and waned in step with the fiscal policies of governments. It declined during periods when free trade was the order of the day, but any Customs dues imposed on a particular commodity quickly revived it, and ensured that commodity being illegally landed in huge quantities, to find a ready market among otherwise respectable citizens. Silks, lace and tea figured largely in contraband cargoes in the days when those items bore high duties and were much in demand, but would hardly be worth smuggling today—just as Swiss watches, since the establishment of EFTA in 1960 and the consequent reduction in import duty, are no longer worth the smuggler's attention. In 1743 it was estimated that duty (then standing at 4s per lb) was collected annually on 650,000lb of tea. The nation's annual consumption was reckoned to be not less than 1,500,000lb. Such was the loss to the Exchequer on one commodity alone.

The period 1700–1850 was one of endless wars for Britain, in her American colonies and with France, Spain and Holland. Many new Customs duties were imposed in order to pay for these wars, and gave rise to a sharp increase in import smuggling, which the government, preoccupied with greater conflicts and unable to spare ships and men, was unable to suppress. In these favourable conditions the smugglers grew bold and prospered. In the words of G. P. R. James, an early nineteenth-century author who wrote of conditions in 1750 or thereabouts:

> Scarcely any one of the maritime countries was in those days without its gang of smugglers; for if France was not opposite, Holland was not far off; and if brandy was not the object, nor silk, nor wine, yet tea or cinnamon, and

hollands, and various East Indian goods were things duly estimated by the British public, especially when they could be obtained without the payment of Custom House dues. The system of prevention also was very inefficient, and a few scattered Custom House officers, aided by a cruiser here or there upon the coast, had an excellent opportunity of getting their throats cut or their heads broken, or of making a decent livelihood by conniving at the transactions they were sent down to stop, as the peculiar temperament of each individual might render such operations pleasant to him. Thus, a roaring trade in contraband goods was going on along the whole British coast, with very little let or hindrance.

The above somewhat sceptical view of the Revenue officer's motivation and apparent lack of zeal was commonplace.

The Customs officers' lot was emphatically not a happy one, and it is remarkable that so many of their number carried out their duties without fear or favour in spite of the personal risk they ran. Popular sentiment was very much on the side of the smuggler. The English have always admired skill and daring at sea, qualities which the old-time smuggler possessed in abundance; but he also had others, less estimable. The ringleaders of the smuggling gangs were often criminals of great depravity, contemptuous of the law and of those in office to uphold it; vicious and brutal even by eighteenth century standards. Their accomplices were the ordinary English people, staunch upholders of individual liberty who regarded any form of taxation as an intolerable encroachment upon it.

The satirist Sydney Smith wrote in 1820 of the outcome of wars:

Taxes are levied upon everything that enters the mouth, covers the back or is placed underfoot; taxes upon everything on earth and on the waters under the earth; on everything from abroad and grown at home; on raw materials and on every fresh value added to it by the industry of man; taxes on the sauce which pampers the rich man's appetite and the drug that restores him to health; on the ermine which decorates the judge and the rope which hangs the criminal; on the poor man's salt and the rich man's spice; on the brass nails of a coffin and the ribbons of a bride . . . The dying Englishman, pouring his medicine, which has paid 7%, into a spoon which has paid 15%, flings himself back on his chintz bed that has paid 22%, makes his will on an eight pound stamp and expires in the arms of an apothecary who has paid one hundred pounds license for the privilege of putting him to death.

Thus the Englishman on taxes, and it was in this atmosphere of general bad odour among his fellow citizens that the Customs officer went about his unpopular and hazardous duties. Just how hazardous they could be on occasion we shall see in due course. Sufficient now to say that bloody pitched battles between the Revenue men and gangs of armed smugglers were commonplace—desperate encounters with desperate men. It was a rare smuggler who gave in without a fight though until 1722 the worst he had to fear was the loss of his ship and cargo, about which he was able to be philosophical, knowing that his losses on one run would be more than covered by his profits on the next. This position was drastically changed, however, by the

Customs Rate Book c 1790, showing the duty payable on various commodities.

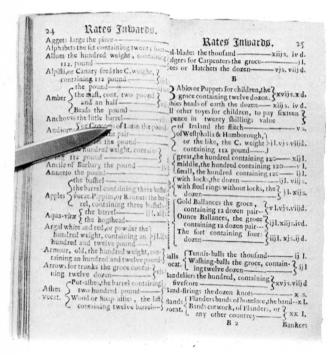

Smugglers Act 1736, when the government, alarmed at the increasing audacity of the smugglers in running their cargoes and their violent resistance to Revenue interference, imposed the death penalty for wounding an officer or for using arms against him; and for resisting unarmed the penalties were transportation, flogging, hard labour, and, perhaps the worst fate, impressment into the fleet. The only noticeable effect this had was to increase the smuggler's resolve not to be taken while he could still fire a pistol or swing a hanger; certainly the rate of contraband-running continued its buoyant upward trend. The reason is not far to seek; the profit to be made on a contraband cargo of tea, brandy, silks, lace or any of the innumerable commodities subject to a high duty was vast, and well worth the not very considerable risk.

Tea, as we have seen, bore a duty of 4s per pound in 1740 or thereabouts. There was a tremendous demand for it; the English were already a tea-drinking nation. Many of the labouring classes drank tea, and that would certainly have been beyond their reach had the tea paid duty. Most of the contraband tea at that time originated in the Dutch East Indies, the English smugglers purchasing their supplies in Holland for as little as 2s per pound and selling it to their more than satisfied customers for between 5s and 7s per pound, depending on quality; this was two or three shillings cheaper than 'legal' tea.

A tub or half-anker of good brandy (four gallons; an anker held about eight Imperial gallons) could be bought in France for as little as 16s. The duty-paid price of brandy in England was about 8s per gallon, so the smuggler could well afford to meet a brisk demand for his wares at 25s the tub and reap a handsome profit. Smuggled rum could be had at 5s a gallon; duty paid, it could not be bought for less than 8s 6d. Port and sherry were freely available at 2s 6d per gallon, whereas no honest wine-merchant, paying duty on his shipments, could afford to sell below 4s. Nor surprisingly, such law-abiding and impoverished traders were few and far between.

Offences.   *Penalties.*

Stat. 13 & 14 *Car.* 2. *cap.* 15. Sect. 7.

— 20 *Car.* 2. *c.* 6. Sect. 3. Confeffion or one Witnefs.

This extends to all Perfons, who fhall imbezil, pawn, or fell, or detain any Silk delivered to any Silk-Manufacturers, Agents, Journeymen, Warpers and Winders, by Stat. 8 & 9 *W.* 3. *c.* 36. Sect. 6.

it not in 14 Days, to be whip'd and fet in the Stocks.

To be committed to Prifon, or Houfe of Correction, till Satisfaction be made or Punifhment inflicted.

Silkthrower.

[Qu. Seff.] Exercifing the Trade of a Silkthrower, not having ferved 7 Years.
Stat. 13 & 14 *Car.* 2. *c.* 15. Sect. 2.

Forty Shillings a Month, one Moiety to the King, the other to the Profecutor.

Smugglers or Runners of foreign Goods.

[Due] After 25 *March* 1722. Perfons, who fhall be found paffing (knowingly and wittingly) with any Foreign Goods or Commodities landed from any Ship or Veffel, without the due Entry and Payment of the Duties, in their Cuftody, from any of the Coafts of this Kingdom, or within twenty Miles of any of the faid Coafts ; and fhall be more than five Perfons in Company, or fhall carry any offenfive Arms or Weapons, or wear any Vizard, Mask, or other Difguife, when paffing with fuch Goods, or fhall forcibly hinder or refift any Officer of the *Cuftoms* or *Excife*, in the feifing Run-Goods.
Stat. 8 *Geo.* 1. *c.* 18. Sect. 6.
Return-

Guilty of Felony, and to be tranfported for feven Years to fome of his Majefty's Plantations or Colonies in *America.*

Felony

Magistrates' Manual of 1722, listing offences and penalties.

H. N. Shore in *Old Foye Days* quotes a master-smuggler on the subject of French brandy:

> The average strength of the liquor supplied was 70 degrees above proof, but I have known cargoes brought over as much as 180 degrees above proof. You see, it was brought over at less expense like that, a hundred tubs making three hundred when mixed to the right strength . . . Of course it required fewer tubs and caused less trouble to the merchant . . . but the mixing gave a lot of trouble. It had to be done after landing, and oftentimes there was a difficulty in getting enough tubs to put the liquor into after it was mixed, so that, on the whole, it gave more trouble than it was worth, in my mind.

The smugglers' difficulties may recall to the reader's memory a recent case where a particularly inept gang of London criminals hijacked a lorry containing several hundred gallons of massively over-proof Scotch whisky. Having sampled the consignment and found it undrinkable in its raw state, they hid it away pending a solution to the problem of dilution. Suspicions were aroused when they began canvassing public houses over a wide area for empty whisky bottles—they apparently did not look the type to be interested in home wine-making—and the police soon picked them up.

When a cargo was landed, some of it would find a home locally, and many of the smugglers' casual helpers, porters and the like, would receive payment in kind. But the bulk of it, naturally, went to large centres of population where customers were thick on the ground and distribution was less of a problem. Much of the contraband landed in the south and south-east found its way to London. Convoys of laden carts and strings of pack-horses regularly made their way across country to the capital, generally moving at dead of night and heavily escorted by hired thugs against the rare contingency of Revenue interference; but few such convoys were troubled, at least until the 1820s, when the Revenue men began to get the upper hand.

The fact was that more often than not the smuggling gangs were so well armed and so outnumbered their adversaries that the latter were forced to hold off and suffer the humiliation of having to watch, from a respectful distance, the goods being run under their very noses. In *Smuggling Days and Smuggling Ways*, H. N. Shore recounts how in June 1744 the officers of the Customs at Eastbourne 'having received intelligence of a gang of smugglers, went, with five dragoons mounted, to the sea-shore, near Pevensey; but one hundred smugglers rode up, and after disarming the officers, fired about forty shots at them, cut them with their swords in a dangerous manner, loaded the goods on above one hundred horses, and made towards London'.

In December 1743, the Margate Surveyor (see glossary) was patrolling with four of his men when they encountered a gang of twenty or so heavily armed smugglers, who promptly set about them. The Revenue men were fortunate to escape with their lives. As it was, one of their number was left with his head 'in such a miserable condition that the Surveyor thought it proper to put him under the care of a Surgeon'. The Surveyor adds that the smugglers customarily went about in large bodies 'who bid defiance to all the officers when they meet'.

The same official had occasion to write to the Board of Customs in April 1746:

> We further beg leave to acquaint your Honours that yesterday about four o'clock in the afternoon a large gang of near 100 smugglers with several lead horses went thro' this town into the island of Thanet, where we hear they landed their goods, notwithstanding that we took all proper care to prevent them.
> PS. This moment we have advice that there is a gang of 200 smugglers more at St Peter's in the Isle of Thanet.

The smugglers' chiefs were not petty malefactors such as were carried off to clink by the parish constable. They were highly organised 'operators', often men of some standing in their own community, who were not regarded by their neighbours (and certainly not by themselves) as anything but upright citizens, performing a public service to the community at large.

They planned their operations carefully, with due regard to the risks involved. In most smuggling ventures, there was an anonymous 'sleeping partner'. He it was who put up the capital and risked his money on the successful outcome. Necessarily a man of means, he was often a citizen of unimpeachable character in his own locality. He might be approached by the master of a smuggling craft and asked to provide the wherewithal to purchase a cargo; assured of handsome returns for his outlay if everything went to plan, he was also assured that in the event of a seizure and prosecution, his part in the matter was never brought to the attention of the magistrates. Indeed, he was as likely as not to be one of their number. His reputation was never at risk, only—sometimes—his cash.

So there was the capital, and the craft to carry the contraband, both under the command of a skilful seaman and smuggler who had his contacts in France and Holland and who could be relied upon to obtain his goods at the best prices and ensure their safe delivery at a time and place of his own choosing.

The other key figure in any smuggling run was the lander. Most of the more notorious personalities of smuggling history were in fact landers: dealers in uncustomed goods rather than smugglers in the true sense. The lander's job, as his name suggests, was to organise the unloading of the contraband from the smuggling craft and its conveyance inland to the distribution point. It was his responsibility to provide labour, pack-ponies and waggons to shift the goods. Half his labour force, which often numbered two hundred or more, was employed to carry the tubs and bales up from the landing-place, load the carts and lead the ponies. The remainder (known as 'batsmen') were armed with cudgels, and not infrequently firearms, and were deployed on both flanks of the landing to present formidable opposition to any Revenue officers bold enough to attempt a seizure.

An essential factor making possible the enormous scale and relative impunity of smuggling operations was the general and active support of the populace at large. The villagers in coastal areas and hinterland provided transport and porterage for the goods, intelligence of local Revenue activity, storage facilities and hiding-places.

H. N. Shore in *Smuggling Days and Smuggling Ways* records the following statement of a witness at an official enquiry:

> The master-smugglers contract for the goods, either abroad, or with the master of a cutter which fetches them, for a quantity of teas (called 'dry goods') and brandies, and the captain of the cutter fixes a time and a place where he designs to land, and seldom or never fails, being pretty punctual as to the time, if the weather permits, as the master-smugglers cannot fetch all the goods themselves, so they hire men whom they call 'riders', and they allow each man half a guinea a journey, and bear all expenses of eating and drinking, and horse, and allowance of a dollop of tea, which is forty pounds weight, being half of a bag, the profit of which dollop, even of the most ordinary sort, is worth more than a guinea, and some 25s, and some more; and they always make one journey, sometimes two, and sometimes three in a week, which is indeed such a temptation that very few people in the country can withstand, and which has been the cause of so many turning.

This somewhat breathless account clearly indicates why farmers in coastal areas were finding themselves short of labour, when agricultural wages amounted to only a few pence daily. A letter in the *Gentleman's Magazine* of September 1735 states: 'In several parts of Kent the farmers are obliged to raise wages, and yet are distressed for want of hands to get in their harvest, which is attributed to the great numbers who employ themselves in smuggling along the coast.' One sympathises with the Kentish farmer in his predicament, and wonders if his dram of uncustomed brandy and pipe of contraband tobacco proved any solace.

In addition to such large-scale operations, a good deal of petty smuggling went on. By the mid-eighteenth century the Continental packet-boat services were well established, notably at Harwich and Dover. Their crews were not averse to a little smuggling, of course, and the packets were rarely stopped and searched en route; it usually • fell to the shore-based Customs officers to rummage these craft on arrival. Many seizures of contraband were made, but as may be expected they were mostly small individual caches of high-duty goods, stowed aboard perhaps without the master's knowledge or consent.

About this time also significant numbers of seizures began to be made from passengers; ordinary citizens who had travelled to the Continent on business or pleasure and took the opportunity to stock up with a few luxuries at advantageous prices. Smuggling by passengers, however, would provide rich material for another book. Women do not figure largely in Revenue histories; the occasional virago appears in records as a member of a gang but it seems likely that the preventive officers had little experience of dealing with 'lady' smugglers. On the rare occasions when they did so their reports reveal that they were scandalised and more than a little embarrassed by the circumstances in which they found themselves. Here is a typical example, in the report of the Collector, Harwich, to the Board of Customs:

> We received your Honrs letter of the 22nd ultimate enclosing a memorial from Mrs De Bardieux praying the delivery of some goods seized from her on her arrival here in a Pacqt. Boat from Holland and complaining of some indecent treatment from the officers . . . we called upon the officers for an acct. of their behaviour to this woman . . . and we found that there was no indecencys acted but by herself. For when the tyde-surveyor found that she had something concealed in her stays, she took him round the neck and held and kiss'd him a considerable time in the presence of several people. And when Mr. Olibar and Mr. Pulham went to her to the Publick House and aquainted her they had an information that she had some prohibited goods concealed about her she immediately lifted up her petticoats to her waist so that her whole behaviour while here was very like a common strumpet . . .

It seems that the Surveyor in this instance could not bring himself to do his duty in front of vulgar onlookers and sent his subordinates to effect the seizure in a less public place; a decision of which the Board no doubt wholly approved.

The smugglers did not always have it all their own way. Occasionally, outraged authority exerted itself to some effect. Shortly before Christmas 1784, a directive went out to all Collections (see glossary) that on Christmas Eve a search was to be made of creeks and inlets for smuggling craft; all such were to be seized and 'to prevent them being launched into the water, and carried off by the smugglers after seizure, you are to cause one of the streaks [ie strakes or planks] to be ripped off near the keel, taking care at the same time to do as little other injury to each boat as possible'. The operation was to be carried out simultaneously all along the coastline during the ensuing twenty-four hours. It was assumed, no doubt, that the smugglers would be off their guard during the Christmas festivities.

Another notable coup on the government's part was staged at Deal, Kent, that town of notorious revenue reputation, in January 1788. On the instructions of no less a person that Prime Minister William Pitt, a regiment of infantry was quartered there, the officers having previously received secret orders. The morning after their arrival the troops were drawn up on the beach. The smugglers' boats were all around, high and dry. Their owners stood about, idle onlookers at what they took to be routine military toing and froing. At a prearranged signal the soldiers broke formation, each squad running to the nearest boat, pouring pitch over it and setting it on fire. The outraged but impotent smugglers, outnumbered for once, could only stand and watch their precious boats burn.

On occasion the Revenue officers, perhaps having prior warning of a run, would contrive to be in the right place at the right time and in sufficient strength to overpower them, or at least to hold them off long enough to seize the goods. The assistance of a detachment of dragoons would sometimes be enlisted, in areas where the military were quartered. But that these forays did not always meet with complete success is scarcely surprising when one considers the handicaps under which the officers laboured. Informers, though not unknown, were rare birds indeed. The smuggling chieftains were the Mafia of their day; the life of a 'traitor' was not worth a tallow dip. The official in charge of such an operation would often find it necessary to denude

The smuggler's grave: headstone in the churchyard at Binstead, Isle of Wight.
The inscription reads 'To the Memory of Thos. Sivell who was cruelly shot on
board his sloop by some officers of the customs of the port of Portsmouth on the
15th of June 1785 at the Age of 64 Years leaving a disconsolate Widow & family'.
The carved relief depicts the fatal encounter.

neighbouring districts of their preventive patrols in order to muster a large enough force to tackle a gang, even when granted the co-operation of a sometimes reluctant military. Then he would have the difficult task of moving his men across country to the suspected landing-place without alerting the smugglers or their friends—and that, of course, included virtually every local inhabitant. For this reason, such movements usually took place under cover of darkness or, if by day, in ones and twos along little-frequented byways.

However, let us assume that all these difficulties were overcome, complete surprise achieved, the smugglers routed, and the contraband seized. The Revenue officers disperse to their various stations, feeling, we may suppose, that satisfaction engendered by the knowledge of duty done. This was sometimes premature. One or more of the smugglers, resisting lawful arrest with a weapon in his hand, might have been shot down during the *mêlee*, or have died subsequently from wounds received. A coroner's jury in the neighbourhood, consisting largely or wholly of smugglers and their associates, would then, more often than not, return a verdict of murder against the long-suffering Crown servants.

During the passage through Parliament of the Smuggling Bill 1736, previously referred to, it was stated:

> In some parts of the maritime counties the whole people are so generally engaged in smuggling that it is impossible to find a jury that will, upon trial, do justice to an officer of the revenue in any case whatever. In those counties where smuggling has become general, the majority of the coroner's inquests always consist of smugglers, so that it has been found by experience that these inquests always bring the officer and his assistants in guilty of murder, even though it be made clearly to appear, by the most undoubted testimonies, that the killing happened *de defendendo*.

The officers concerned were usually acquitted at the resultant trial, but that did little to diminish their sense of outrage at being put in peril of their lives for doing their duty.

Brewery 4/Page 131
Feb. 24 & 5t
No return shewn on warm
worts that evening. —
In B.ry, page 131, a
Charge not set forward.
In D.; page 133, a Charge
not set forward. —
In D.o 134, a Charge not
set forward. —
In D.o page 128, an
increase of Stock, two
firkins of a, not set
forward. —
Stock book, page 106
From Feb. 23 to March
3, stock one day wide

162 - 18. 0 - 8. 2
160 - 120. 0 - 8. 2

Dryffeholm
27 & 1
& 3 Dockerbie
2 Wine D. rs
2 Sh.t D. rs
3 Tea D. rs
3 Tob. D. rs
& 6

55. 5
73. 1
128. 6

71. 4
125. 5

Robert Burns' survey book, recording his supervision of Excise officers in his
district.

Description	Name	£	s	d		Notes
can do, gwen to drink	Coen Bigg	37	16	6		36, 94.
but middling drinks	Js.t Boyd	39	18	5		207, 207, 212, 107
a good off.r	Alex.r Bowes Sen	61	33	3		210. Dear
but Indifferent	Wm Bruce	43	16	6		116.
a good off.r	Alex Bowes Jun	35	7	1		96.
a blundering off.r	John Bruce Esq.	37	9	7		116, 118.
a good off.r	Robt Blakey	31	7	3		94.
a good off.r	Alex.r Brown Esq	39	10	6		124.
a good off.r & liquoremaker	And.w Benny Sen	32	7	3		118
makes a good off.r	Alex.r Bayne Esq	32	7	5		182.
a weak man but sober	James Buchanan	33	7	1.		104
a carefull off.r	And.w Brodie	32	8	1		84.
a carefull good off.r	John Burnet	38	9	2		116.
a good off.r	James Booth	37	9	4		118
The Poet, does pretty well	Robert Burns	32	3	7		94.
a good off.r	Wm Brown	28	5	3		96
	John Black	33	6	3		96.
a good off.r	Robt Barclay	41	12			82
a good off.r	Alex.r Bruce	28	5	1		98, 96
a weak man, but Sober	Wm Bowman	30	6	4		86, 118
Sober & attentive but weak	John Brodie					108, 106.
	Jas Butchart					
but Indifferent	Arch Brodee					
Sober & Attentive	Geo. Balvaird	32	3	1		124.
	Geo. Brown	29	6	1		120,
	And.w Benny Jun					
makes a good off.r	Jas Blatson					126
	Tho.s Black					
Sober & carefull	Ralph Birrel					
Pretty attentive	Jas Burley					
	Wm Beatie					
	Wm Brand					

A page from the Staff and Wages register kept by Burns' superior at Dumfries. Burns is described as 'The Poet; does pretty well'. His salary was £32 3s 7d per annum.

It may seem cause for wonder that men were found to staff the Revenue. Such posts were in fact much sought after. Salaries were respectable by the standards of the day, and by 1820 pensions were being granted. Some secured appointments in inland areas where the smugglers were comparatively inactive, and where nothing more was expected of the officer than a nominal attendance at his place of duty and the ability to get on with his neighbours. Robert Burns, for instance, was appointed to the Excise in Dumfriesshire in 1789, and served there until his death in 1796. He found time to write poetry (it was his most prolific period) and also to pursue his social activities as a lionised literary figure.

A further and considerable incentive to recruitment was the system under which rewards were paid to officers responsible for effecting seizures, proportionate to the value of the goods seized. Some idea of what this could mean to an official with a salary of £30–40 a year is shown by the seizure of a large quantity of tea and spirits made by a humble tide-waiter (see glossary) in 1786. His share of the reward was no less than £3,000—a considerable fortune by any standards in those days. This was exceptional, of course, but substantial sums could be earned often enough by a reasonably diligent officer.

A manpower crisis in the Revenue service did exist, however, because the nation was perpetually fighting wars, or on the brink of war, and the Customs had low priority.

2

The Revenue Cutters

Mr. Sarmon of the *Swan Revenue* cutter having represented to us that in the last skirmish, the smugglers took away from his boat's crew 12 pistols, 9 cutlasses and 4 muskets, we humbly pray your Honors will order the same number to supply the place of those that are lost.

Letter to the Board, June 1784

It might be labouring the obvious to suggest that the first line of defence against the smuggling hordes should have been located as an effective maritime force, in those narrow waters of the Channel, Old England's famous moat, which had so often in the past deterred undesirables. In fact, an impoverished Treasury were content for the most part to leave the establishment and maintenance of the sea-borne Revenue force to private enterprise; a system which bred its own evils, as we shall see. In 1703, there were just eight Revenue craft in service to guard the coastline from the Bristol Channel to the North Foreland.

From Charles II's reign there had been a few 'Custom House smacks', usually hired at major ports, which were employed to patrol anchorages, board inbound vessels and inspect bills of lading. They also made some attempt to check wool smuggling, but with little success.

Under William III it was enacted (7 & 8 Wm III, c 28; author's italics):

> that for the better preventing the exportation of wool and correspondence with France . . . the Lord High Admiral of England . . . shall *from time to time* direct and appoint one ship of the Fifth Rate, and two ships of the Sixth Rate, and four armed sloops constantly to patrol off the North Foreland to the Isle of Wight, with orders for taking and seizing all ships, vessels or boats which shall export wool or carry or bring any prohibited goods or *any suspected persons.*

Thus, for the first time, the assistance of men-of-war was enlisted specifically in suppressing the smuggling trade. Note that the government was already concerned about the concomitant of smuggling; a two-way seditious traffic of specie outwards, Jacobite spies inwards and correspondence both ways. Note also that the king's ships were to be made available only when they could be spared from their war stations. This spasmodic co-operation was reciprocated; the coastline was further stripped of Revenue protection on the occasions when some of the few cutters in commission were withdrawn to act as tenders to the fleet.

At the beginning of the eighteenth century the preventive service, afloat and on shore, was the responsibility of the Board of Customs. It remained so until well after the Napoleonic Wars, being taken over in 1831 by the Royal Navy's newly-formed Coastguard Service. Few of the cutters in service up to the middle of the eighteenth century were owned and maintained wholly by the Board of Customs. The majority were provided by outside contractors, in exchange for a share in the profits arising from seizures. These could be considerable, as we have seen. The procedure was as follows: the seized goods, together with the vessel in which they were carried, were 'condemned' and subsequently sold to the highest bidder. Of the proceeds, half went to the Exchequer as the 'king's share'; the other half was divided between the contractor and the crew of the Revenue cutter according to rank.

The contract system was lax and open to abuse. The contractor did not, as a rule, have any zeal for the Revenue; his sole object was to make a profit from seizure rewards whilst keeping expenditure on the cutter to a minimum. Some contractors were shown in articles as the commander, but would send their cutters cruising under the mate and go about their own affairs, not failing to claim a share on any seizures got, even though not present at the time.

Such a lack of dedication on the contractor's part was not wholly inexcusable, for the Board of Customs at that time was a notoriously untrustworthy and devious employer. Captain Robinson of the *Spye*, a Revenue cruiser based on the north-east coast, made in 1725 a very commendable seizure of a Dutch dogger off Hull with a cargo of 180 casks of brandy, whereupon the Board, ever timid in enforcing their powers of seizure, informed him that unless he was prepared to bring a private prosecution, he should restore the seizure. Not surprisingly, Captain Robinson would have none of this, and he informed the Board as recorded in the Board of Customs Letter Book, port of Hull, 1725: 'I'll not stand tryal at my own charge, and I've sent to Mr Grant, ye Dutch merchant's Solicitor to know how he would propose to bring ye Matter to an amicable Agreement. His answer shall be handed to your Honble Board, on whom I shall throw myself entirely, to be made clear of all Charge, litigious Cavill & law-suit, for I have done no more than my duty in bringing ye vessel in your suspicion.'

Though not all the faults were on the contractors' side, the system was unsatisfactory. Moreover, a situation where many cutter commanders were rarely seen on board by their crews could not be allowed to continue. A disciplinary inquiry involving such an absentee commander, held in 1787, led to the ending of the system in the following year. Thereafter, until the Royal Navy took over in 1831, the Revenue fleet was both owned and administered by the Board of Customs.

Not all the old contract cutters were inefficient, as we have already seen in the case of *Spye*. Some cutters were owned by the local Collec-

The view across to East Cowes and William Arnold's residence.

tor of Customs, who acted as contractor, and was careful to keep the
commander and crew up to the mark. One such was the *Swan*, based at
Cowes, Isle of Wight. This craft was built by William Arnold (father of
Dr Thomas Arnold of Rugby School) who was Collector at Cowes
from 1777 to 1801, and built at his own expense, with the sanction of
the Commissioners, as a financial venture. He certainly did not make a
fortune, despite the exertions of a very capable commander, for

unluckily the first *Swan* was wrecked in a gale after only a few months' service. There were to be four more of that name, however, but only *Swan* I and II were contracted to Arnold. When the contract system was ended in 1788 *Swan* II was put on the Customs establishment.

Mr Arnold had other sources of income, stemming from the activities of various men-of-war operating against the smugglers within his Collection. 'This week has produced the condemnation of the *Orestes*' prize. I propose selling the cutter and above 2,000 gallons of spirits seized with her, which with nine tons of tea, I think must produce me a commission of at least £150', he wrote in 1784. (Arnold's salary at this time was £155 3s 4d per annum.)

Revenue cutters are generally referred to in contemporary records as 'cruisers', regardless of build or rig. In fact they were for the most part cutters, sloop-rigged and clinker-built (see glossary) for stoutness— a very necessary quality when crashing alongside a fleeing smuggler to grapple and board him. The cutter was a characteristically English type; single-masted, with two head sails and a bowsprit which could be run in and out. Another distinctive feature was the broad, flat counter. At their best they achieved a fine balance between strength and speed. Speed was essential. The smugglers, with no shortage of funds for building, also favoured the sloop-rig cutter as the fastest and handiest. In addition, their superb boats were often carvel-built (see glossary), the smooth hull more fragile but having less water-resistance: an extra knot or two made all the difference between ignominious capture and a clean pair of heels in the days of muzzle-loading guns with an effective range of only a few hundred yards.

Keble-Chatterton gives us a good description of a typical Revenue cutter of the period in *King's Cutters and Smugglers* (see illustration opposite, also p 55):

> Those for the Customs service, being required to keep the sea for long periods in all weathers, had to be far more stoutly built than the smuggler's vessels that could pick time and place for their short runs. Yet in spite of this, the

Revenue craft required, if possible, more speed than the lightly-built smugglers. Hence were evolved heavy craft of low freeboard and great depth of keel, with enormous sail area for their size. The low deck level was made up for high bulwarks pierced for guns, and a raised foredeck with bold sheer up to great bluff bows. Like everything else about these vessels, the mast was stout and heavy. A straight bowsprit almost as long as the hull was fitted to run in and out. The foot of the great gaff-mainsail hauled out to a driver boom reaching far outside the taffrail, a spar introduced with a view to speed.

The long bowsprit referred to made possible a great spread of jib-sails, characteristic of the Revenue cutter. It was known as the 'illegal bowsprit' because the fitting of such was forbidden by law to any but a Revenue craft or a man-of-war. There were smugglers, needless to say, who attempted to find a way round this restriction.

Authentic model of a Revenue cutter c 1800, showing details of spars, rigging and armament.

In a letter to the Board, dated 1786, William Arnold wrote:

> No person who has seen the vessel in question, altho' her bowsprit is fixed and of the legal length which all vessels' bowsprits are required to be, has ever thought of calling her anything but a cutter, and we believe a more handsome cutter or one better calculated for fast sailing never went to sea. That she is intended for smuggling there can be no doubt. The principal owner is a notorious smuggler, and during the time he has been fitting her out we have had cause to be arrested one of the men belonging to her, a noted smuggler by the name of Black Jack.
>
> All which circumstances, added to the cutter's having a large tub boat such as is used only in the smuggling trade, have induced me to stop her proceeding to sea until we could state the case and have your directions for our future government.

The inspection and licensing of small craft by the Board of Customs was a measure aimed at the smugglers, intended to hamper their building and operating craft of a size and speed equal to or surpassing that of the Revenue cutters. Any vessel caught running without a licence, or with its fittings significantly altered after licensing, was liable to seizure, whether or not it was carrying contraband. Not all small-boat owners were smugglers, of course, any more than they are today, and some of them strongly resented their craft being seized on what they regarded as specious and pettifogging grounds. There were many other restrictions apart from the length of bowsprit, such as hull dimensions and size of sail area. Even the number of oars fitted in an open boat could constitute an infringement, as laid down in an Act of 1721:

> Any boat built to row with more than four oars, found upon land or water within the counties of Middlesex, Surrey, Kent or Sussex, or in the River Thames, or within the limits of the port of London, Sandwich, or Ipswich, or any boat rowing with more than six oars found either upon land or water, in any other port, or within two leagues of the coast of Great Britain, shall be forfeited, and any person using or rowing in such boat shall forfeit £40.

Such was the law, but there were ways and means of evading it. Arnold-Foster (see bibliography, p 149) quotes the following passage from a letter to the Board, dated June 1784:

> Mr. Sarmon reports that the persons who were standing by the boat when he came up with her had bludgeons in their hands, but on his getting more assistance from his cutter they no otherwise obstructed him in seizing the boat than by greatly abusing him.
>
> One of the bludgeons being left in the boat appeared to have been used as a stretcher for the persons rowing to place their feet against, and it is more than probable that they were intended to be used occasionally for that purpose, or as weapons of offence against the officers.
>
> The boat measured 40 ft. in length and only 4 ft. 10 inches in breadth. We pray your directions for prosecuting the same to condemnation.

In view of the last paragraph, the infringement in this case was presumably the boat's dimensions. The suspected use of the 'bludgeons' as extra stretchers is significant; additional thwarts and rowlocks could also be unshipped without leaving obvious traces, to conceal the use of an illegal number of oars.

A further measure intended to restrict the smugglers' activities was the statute of 1718, known as the 'Hovering Act', under which any sailing vessel of less than 200 tons burthen could be seized if found, without reasonable cause, outside the limits specified on its licence— normally three leagues (about nine land miles) from the coast, though this limit was varied from time to time.

It will be seen that there was no lack of anti-smuggling legislation; the problem was to catch the transgressor. The smugglers generally confined their operations to the winter months, accepting the greater danger and hardship of crossings in winter gales in exchange for the lesser risk of capture during long hours of darkness and foul weather when the Revenue cutters, regrettably, were wont to skulk in harbour. Also, the smuggler chose his time and place to make a run, and with local intelligence at his disposal was able to take advantage of any temporary direction of Revenue forces to another district. Even when unlucky enough to encounter a Revenue cutter, many smuggling craft were capable of out-sailing or out-gunning their adversaries.

In June 1784 Arnold described in a report to the Board of Customs the audacity of smugglers in attacking a man-of-war's boat, killing one bluejacket and wounding two others. The boat belonged to the *Orestes*, a fast cutter captured from the Dutch, and one of the king's ships employed in the Revenue service, at the time under Arnold's control. The smuggling craft which fired upon them was reported to be armed with twenty-two guns on deck, and, said Arnold: 'As this is another instance added to the many which occur almost daily of the outrageous and piratical proceedings of the smugglers on this coast, we think it our duty to represent the same to your Honors.'

A few months previously, Arnold had been moved to write to the Board:

> We beg leave to report that within the last three years smuggling has increased upon this coast to an alarming degree. Illicit trade is principally carried on in large armed cutters or luggers from two to three hundred tons burthen, with which the Revenue cruisers are not able to contend. It is no unusual thing for them to land their goods in open day under protection of their guns, sometimes in sight of Revenue cutters whom they will not suffer to come near or board them.
>
> The war [ie the American War of Independence] gave a sanction to the arming of these vessels, as the masters took out commissions as privateers, tho' in fact they followed no other trade than smuggling. Now the war is over they continue their illicit practices.
>
> These large vessels frequently convoy over other smaller ones. They keep off until towards night, when they run in and land their cargoes at places where gangs of smugglers sometimes to the number of 200–300 meet them.
>
> Goods are often landed out of large deep boats carrying 500–1000 casks which have been unshipped at sea from the importing vessels. As soon as seen by a Revenue cruiser, they drop the boat astern, which immediately rows off while the commander of the Revenue cutter is pursuing the vessel he supposes to be loaded. When he comes up, to his disappointment, he finds no cargo on board . . .

It seems the smugglers were capable of guile as well as armed resistance; though it would be surprising if the decoy trick worked more than once.

From time to time, the Commissioners had reason to be disturbed at an apparent lack of zeal and enterprise on the part of some civilian cutters' crews, as a later chapter will show (see p 50). The Board's letter-books of the 'civilian' period contain many examples of exhortations and admonishments directed at the commanders. It can be said in their defence that the smuggler held most of the tricks; theirs was not an enviable task and morale was generally low in the cutter service.

The crew of a Revenue cutter consisted of a commander, a mate—sometimes two in the bigger craft—and a number of mariners, depending on its size. The commander and the mates held commissions as Customs officers by virtue of their posts. In addition, one or two of the crew would be similarly appointed; they were known as 'deputed mariners'. A lot of preventive work was carried out in open boats away from the parent vessel and it was necessary that there should always be one member of a boat's crew who was authorised to act as an officer of Customs, in order legally to detain and search vessels, and to seize contraband.

Aspects of Revenue Work

We have gathered that some civilian commanders fell short on diligence and revenue zeal. It should be added that a few of them, in unsought encounters with the more aggressive smugglers, revealed themselves to be lacking the ordinary courage which might have been taken for granted in men of their calling. There were a number of instances where Revenue cutters deliberately avoided a fight, not merely when discretion was the better part of valour (as was sometimes the case when the cutter was outgunned) but because valour was altogether lacking.

Not the first incident of this kind, but surely the worst, involved the cutter *Swan* of Cowes, the fifth of that name (see p 36). Her predecessors had done sterling work under their commander Francis Sarmon, whose exploits we shall hear more of. He was slain in the course of a gun battle with a French privateer in 1796, while commanding *Swan IV*.

Old: Revenue cutter *Repulse* in chase of a lugger . . .
. . . and New: HMRC *Valiant* at speed.

E. Keble-Chatterton (*King's Cutters and Smugglers*) describes how on 19 March 1807, *Swan V*, under the command of one Richard Comben (erstwhile mate to Captain Sarmon) was cruising off the Needles when she fell in with three smuggling luggers. The wind had dropped, and the smugglers had sweeps out. Comben made no attempt to close with them, but stood off, wringing his hands. 'It is all over with us', he was heard to remark despairingly to one of his crew, who was urging him to bring up ammunition. Despite their craven commander, the crew put up a stalwart fight for three-quarters of an hour, and they were still at their quarters when Comben hailed the luggers: 'Leave off firing, I have struck.' At this, not surprisingly, the cutter's men gave in, and taking to the boats, rowed ashore. The smugglers captured the *Swan* and carried her off to France, together with her commander, who returned to England seven years later to face disgrace and dismissal.

It seems that Comben commanded a better crew than he deserved. However, there was some excuse when crews showed a lack of resolution in pressing an attack on a formidable opponent for until 1808 there was no provision for the payment of compensation for injuries received on duty. In that year a scale of payments was introduced under which a mariner was paid a pension of £10 per annum for the loss of a limb; the Crown also undertook to foot the bill when the services of a surgeon were necessary; and, in addition, pensions were paid to the widows and orphans of men killed in action against smugglers. This scheme proved to be of more benefit to the Revenue than any amount of exhortation.

Despite the disagreeable aspects of Revenue work, there was never any shortage of recruits to man the cutters; indeed, interest in high places was often necessary to secure a berth in the humblest capacity. Pay and conditions compared favourably with those in the merchant service, without the disadvantage for a family man of long deep-sea voyages, and we have seen that large sums could sometimes be earned in seizure rewards. Another considerable inducement was the exemption from impressment enjoyed by cutters' men.

During the Napoleonic wars no trained seaman—or able-bodied landsman for that matter—was safe from the press gang. The mariner joining a cutter was furnished with a written 'protection' which he was always to carry with him when ashore, on duty or off.

Samuel Stokes, a merchant seaman, wrote in his journal in 1809:

> I went to Harwich with several more and shipped at Harwich Custom House to go on board the *Rattlesnake* on the Revenue Service. She was lying at Deptford fitting out, and the latter part of the week I was sent with several more to join the *Rattlesnake* at Deptford. I got a good protection when I joined this vessel. I could go ashore or anywhere I pleased without being afraid of being pres'd.

A surviving example of one of these protections reads as follows:

Custom House, London
16 Feby 1808

1808
Protection Customs
By the Commissioners for managing and causing to
be levied and collected His Majesty's Customs.
We do hereby certify that John White whose age and description is at the foot hereof is employed as a mariner on board the ROSE cutter.
W. Warne Johnson, Commander, in the service of His Majesty's Customs.

J. Willis   J. Hurst
J. Munro   J. G. Luttrell

Twenty years of age, five feet four inches high, brown complexion, short brown hair.

If John White were careless enough to leave this document behind he could be picked up by the press during a spell ashore and drafted to a ship of the fleet, his claim to exemption unsupported and therefore disregarded.

But the cutter service was expected to provide seamen for the king's ships, if not always from its own ranks. The Board of Customs stressed to commanders the importance of securing the persons of smugglers for impressment. A quarterly return was called for from each commander, listing among other things the number of smugglers captured and how they were disposed of. In a Treasury minute dated September 1807 commanders were notified that the Lords Commissioners of the Treasury had determined, 'as a further inducement to diligence and activity . . . to grant a reward of £500 to the commander of the Revenue cruiser who, in the course of the year ending 1st October 1808, shall have secured and delivered over to His Majesty's Naval Service the greatest number of smugglers; a reward of £300 to the commander who shall have secured and delivered over the next greatest number, and a reward of £200 for third on the list in those respects'. This top-of-the-league-table bonus was additional to the normal reward of £20 a head for each smuggler pressed into the Navy. The smugglers referred to it contemptuously as 'blood money', and hated their adversaries the more for it, as well they might. Most of them preferred the known rigours of gaol to the uncertainties of naval service.

The Customs and the Navy

After 1816, most of the cutters were commanded by lieutenants of the Navy, of whom there were large numbers reduced to the half-pay list at the ending of the Napoleonic Wars. With the advent of peace and the wholesale paying off of ships in the fleet, the revenue service, despised as it was by the Navy generally, offered the only chance of sea-going employment likely to be had by scores of junior officers without influence and private means. As it was, there were other candidates for the available posts. Some years previously, Rear Admiral Sir Charles Middleton, in a memorandum to Pitt, had recommended the employment of Royal Navy sailing masters in the service, rather than lieutenants: 'They are fewer in number, more roughly educated than lieutenants, and their characters better known; they are the standing pilots, too, of the King's ships, and would be increasing their knowledge in that useful and necessary branch, while they are serving the public in another.' However, with naval unemployment rife, the less 'roughly educated' lieutenants were glad enough to serve the Revenue as cutter commanders, and those worthy warrant officers, the masters, RN, rested content with a mate's berth.

Even an officer of the Royal Navy had no powers to act for the Revenue without a specific authorisation from the Board of Customs; these were issued to individual officers who were from time to time engaged on preventive duties. But by an Act of 1786 (26 Geo III, c 40, s 27) any naval officer afloat was authorised to seize goods, persons and vessels.

Relations between the Customs and the Navy were not cordial. Each was jealous of the rights and privileges enjoyed by the other, particularly in the matter of seizure rewards, prize-money and bounties, which did not make for efficiency on the occasions when the two services were supposed to be co-operating against the smugglers. A minor and somewhat ludicrous manifestation of this ill-feeling throughout the eighteenth century was the continuous dispute over the flying by Revenue cutters of the Customs pendant. This flag was required by law to be hoisted at the masthead of a cutter when giving chase to a suspected smuggler (it is clearly shown in the illustration on p 55) so that the latter should be in no doubt as to the cutter's identity and intent. Its purpose was to forestall any excuses the smuggler might subsequently make for failing to heave to when ordered. With this single exception, only a king's ship in commission was entitled to wear a pendant. Strictly speaking, the cutter was to hoist hers only during the chase and at no other time; the trouble arose because some commanders were in the habit of flying it on less pressing occasions. The long red Revenue banner appeared to provoke naval officers greatly, rather as a similar rag is said to enrage bulls. There occurred more than one incident where the offending strip of bunting was forcibly removed as described in the following report by Captain John Rutter, cutter commander, in 1700:

> He (Admiral Hopson) ordered my pendant to be taken down. I being absent, my men would not do it without my order, whereon he sent his boat on board and one of his men took it down. I coming on board to goe about my duty ordered it to be hoysted again and immediately he sent his boat with one of his Lieutenants to take it down again with a verball order which I refused to let him do, but by strength overpowered me and my company and took it down by force, and beat us to ye degree that I know not whether it may not hazard some men's lives, which I acknowledge I did not wear it in contempt, and if he had sent another time I would readily have obeyed his Order . . .

One likes to imagine the smugglers running a cargo nearby while all this choleric hauling of flag-halliards was going on.

There were other, more serious, matters of contention. Individual men-of-war were from time to time suspected of smuggling; probably with good reason. We have a contemporary account, published in 1835, and written by a bluejacket, 'Jack Nastyface', who served in a warship engaged on blockade duties in the Channel, around 1810:

> On board the different ships, there were numerous packages, which had been shipped at Flushing, and no doubt but they were intended to be smuggled into England from the secret manner, and the different stratagems used, in the getting of them afterwards on shore. The bread-room of our ship was crowded with them, directed for different officers holding high rank, both in army and navy, and may have been intended as presents or for their own use, but they did not pay the duty . . . Not being able to land all these goods at once without detection, we contrived it at different intervals, safely thus got rid of some of them by different conveyances and then we became 'Channel Gropers' again, and whilst on duty we landed the balance of our secret cargo, at Weymouth and Plymouth, as we were frequently running into these ports. Whilst on the Cherbourg blockade station, it often occurred that we were in chase of vessels supposing them to be smugglers, and at the same time, we were meditating how to get rid of the bulk of our breadroom stowage which did not intend to pay any duty, for we had His Majesty's pendant which no custom-house officer searches so strictly . . .
> It would savour more of propriety if the revenue officers were a little more vigilant, and kept an eye on those who are paid to prevent infractions, instead of being the first violators of our laws.

The Revenue Cutters

'Jack Nastyface', whose true identity has not been established, has the reputation among naval historians of being something of a sea-lawyer. He rarely has a good word to say of his officers, certainly, but this is hardly surprising as he speaks as a pressed seaman enduring the brutal lower-deck conditions of Nelson's navy. However, we have little reason to doubt his allegations of smuggling on the part of Royal Navy officers. Many other instances came to light. On one occasion a ship of the fleet was caught red-handed with contraband spirits on board and actually seized by an over-zealous Customs official. But the seizure of a king's ship on behalf of the Crown was patently inadmissible, and the vessel was hastily released by an embarrassed Board of Customs.

Incidents of this sort did little to improve relationships, and bad feeling between the Revenue service and the Royal Navy persisted until 1816, when the Admiralty took over the administration and manning of the cutters. For a lively (if somewhat libellous) description of the scene on board a Revenue cutter in the eighteen-twenties, we turn to Captain Marryat, who writes in his novel *Two Cutters:*

She is a cutter, and you may know she belongs to the Preventive Service by the number of gigs and galleys which she has hoisted up all round her. She looks like a vessel that was about to sail with a cargo of boats: two on deck, one astern, one on each side of her. You observe that she is painted black, and all her boats are white. She is not such an elegant vessel as the yacht, and she is much more lumbered up . . . Let us go on board, and her bulwarks are painted red; it is not a very becoming colour, but then it lasts a long while, and the dockyard is not very generous on the score of paint—or lieutenants of the navy troubled with much spare cash. She has plenty of men, and fine men they are; all dressed in red flannel shirts and blue trousers; some of them have not taken off their canvas or tarpaulin petticoats, which are very useful to them, as they are in the boats night and day, and in all weathers. But we will at once go down into the cabin, where we shall find the lieutenant who commands her, a master's mate, and a midshipman. They each have their tumbler before them, and are drinking gin-toddy, hot, with sugar—capital gin, too—'bove proof; it is from that small anker standing under the table. It is one that they forgot to return to the Custom House when they made their last seizure.

The colour-scheme described is broadly that which was standard for the smaller warships of the period. As for the crew, it appears that they were rigged out in a uniform of sorts—perhaps at their commander's expense, as a uniform for ratings in the Navy was not introduced until 1857. The commander and officers would, of course, be wearing the naval uniform appropriate to their rank.

Before 1816 the commander and mates were usually civilians, members of a semi-civilian service, but customarily wore a uniform when on duty. The precise form that this took in pre-naval days has been difficult to establish from records of the time, but the following specification provides a reasonably accurate picture. In a petition to the Board, dated June 1804, the commanders suggested for themselves: 'A silver epaulette, the button-holes worked or bound with silver twist or lace, side-arms, and cocked hats with cockades, and the buttons set on the coat three and three, the breeches and waistcoats as usual'. They also proposed a new uniform for the mates, differing slightly from their own in detail. The design was approved by the Board, with the exception of the epaulette. This particular adornment had only recently been granted to officers of the Royal Navy, who were not inclined to share the distinction with Customs officers.

Later, in 1842, the regulation uniform for civilian cutter commanders consisted of a blue frock-coat with a high collar decorated with a loop of gold braid and a button (similar to that of a modern naval cadet). The lapels were buttoned back with a row of Coastguard uniform buttons, and there were three buttons on each cuff. The cocked hat had been replaced by a peaked cap of blue cloth, trimmed with gold braid. The commander and mates wore swords, complete with sword-knot and belt of black leather. Their uniform was similar to that of a junior naval officer of the period—always excepting, of course, the epaulette.

3

Some Shortcomings

Amongst the papers brought in by the *Wasp*, sloop-of-war, was enclosed letter from Mr. Weston to John Early, a smuggler of great notoriety and property, giving an account of the military force stationed at Poole.

The very strong similitude between the writing of the name 'Weston' in the letter and the signature of the Comptroller of Poole on several dispatches from that port, leads us to apprehend that he may have been so imprudent as to give intelligence to Early of the soldiers quartered there to act against the smugglers.

Letter to the Board of Customs, July 1798

It was apparent that on certain parts of the coast, the smugglers enjoyed a markedly greater freedom of movement than was the case elsewhere. Allegations were made in particular localities of collusion between smugglers and revenue officers. Some writers of Customs histories have implied that corruption in the preventive service was the general rule. What evidence there is does not bear this out, but it would be idle to pretend that all Customs officers were incorruptible in an era when any public office, high or low, was regarded as a licence for jobbery. For every charge of collusion which was proved, however, there were a dozen which were merely malicious rumours put about by disgruntled citizens. It would be no exaggeration to say that for most of the eighteenth century half the population were either actively engaged in smuggling or deriving benefit from it by their access to uncustomed goods. It is not surprising, therefore, that the agents of the Revenue were thoroughly detested; a smuggler ready to give a Revenue man his due was as rare as a modern motorist willing to acknowledge the usefulness of traffic wardens.

The cutters did not escape the taint of corruptibility, although there is no record of a proven instance so far as they were concerned. Such a charge must have been difficult of proof, in any case. The fact that a particular cutter was habitually conspicuous by its absence from the scene of a run could have been due to various causes, and was not necessarily incriminating. However, it was undeniable that some cutters had a very poor seizure record even in areas where smugglers were active, which could indicate either collusion or sheer inertia, perhaps both.

A Mr Lisle reported to the Home Secretary, Lord Shelburne, on 8 August 1782 (*Shelburne Papers*, Vol. III):

> Two Revenue Cutters to guard this station [from the Isle of Wight to St Alban's Head]. That from Southampton makes some good Seizures the other from Poole very few, and I am well informed, owing to the Master Mate & Crews being corrupted, and on certain signals now in my possession, the latter withdraws to another part of the Coast, to give opportunitys to the Smugglers to land, and carry off their Cargoes; without interruption, tho' sometimes, they are bribed with a few Casks, to save appearances . . .

Pure hearsay this, presumably; Mr Lisle does not provide his noble employer with concrete facts.

In the mid-eighteenth century, smuggling was particularly rife in Cornwall and it was generally assumed by non-Cornishmen that some of the local preventive men were in the pay of the free-traders. This may or may not have been the case; certainly it is understandable if the preventives chose not to antagonise their adversaries more than they could help. These men were also their neighbours, and in some cases their relatives, or their wives' relatives. Many of the gamekeepers came of poacher stock! In addition, the cutter crews, at least, had arduous work to do, dangerous on occasion but mostly monotonous, with endless patrols in foul weather, cramped quarters and little time ashore. Small wonder if they were tempted now and then to find a snug anchorage for the night and let the smugglers do their worst.

However, changes were about to be made in those remote parts. In 1769 the Commissioners appointed a new broom, Mr Samuel Pellew (brother of the famous admiral), to the Collectorship at Falmouth. Before long, he was to make his presence felt by smugglers and Revenue staff alike.

There were two cutters based at Falmouth; the *Hawk* and the *Lark* and under Mr Pellew's new regime both of them were kept constantly cruising on station; so much so that the commander of one resigned his post in disgust. The smugglers did not take kindly to this unwonted activity either. The new Collector was several times threatened with dire retribution, and this was no empty threat in an age when no agent of the Revenue, however elevated, was exempt from the risk of personal assault. But Pellew was not the man to be turned aside from duty. Slowly but steadily, under his leadership, the preventive forces in Cornwall gained the upper hand.

Pellew personally led a successful foray against the most notorious smuggler in his area, one Wellard, owner and skipper of the *Happy-go-Lucky* cutter and an outlawed criminal who had sworn on many occasions that he would never be taken alive. Having information of Wellard's whereabouts, the redoubtable Collector embarked in the *Lark* cutter, to ensure that her crew exerted themselves; his brother, then a half-pay Captain, RN, who happened to be at home at the time, took passage in the *Hawk*. The two cutters sailed in company, and on 4 April 1786 surprised their quarry at anchor in Mount's Bay. *Hawk*, being the faster of the two, fetched up first with the *Happy-go-Lucky*. She fought a fierce gun-action with the smuggler for half an hour;

To Captain Bursack on board Speedwell
revenue Cutter now lying at Fordingbridge

Sir,
        Damn thee
and God Damn thy two Purblind Eyes thou
Buger and thou Death looking son of a Bitch
O that I had bin there (with my company)
for thy sake when thou tookes them men of
Mine on Board the Speedwell Cutter on Monday
the 14 Decr I would cross thee and all thy
Gang to Hell wher thou belongest thou
Devil Incarnet. Go Down thou Hell Hound
into thy Kennell below & Bathe thy
Self in that Sulpherous Lake that has
bin so long Prepared for such as thee for
it is time the World was rid of such a
Monster thou art no Man but a Devil
thou fiend O Lucifer I hope thou will
soon fall into Hell like a star from the
Sky; there to lie (unpitied) & unrelented of any
for Ever & Ever Which God Grant of his
Infinite Mercy Amen
                    J. Spurier
Fordingbridge Jan 32 1700 & fast asleep

Copied from original found in Poole
            Custom House

Cutter commander's fan mail.

then the *Lark* came up and raked the cornered craft from astern with a fusillade of grape-shot along her deck. Wellard was killed outright, thereby making good his boast; several of his crew were wounded and the rest surrendered.

The survivors were taken ashore and lodged in Pendennis Castle, from whence they were shortly afterwards rescued by the townsfolk. Only one stood trial (he was too badly wounded to be carried to safety with the rest) but was duly acquitted by the customary smuggler's jury. Aside from the disheartening sequel, this punitive expedition proved that, given efficient organisation and determined leadership, the cutters were well able to give an account of themselves. A lot depended upon the calibre of the Collector, and in areas where this important post was filled by men of the stamp of Pellew, the smugglers learned to be wary. His subordinates, too, were made amply aware of what was expected of them, and that any suspicion of collusion on their parts would lead to instant dismissal.

It will be understood that it was unusual for a Collector to direct such an operation in person; indeed, most Collectors would have been appalled at the suggestion. Translated into military terms, Mr Pellew's action was that of a general leading a raid into No Man's Land. Possibly it was Captain Pellew who put his brother up to it. This escapade must have made a welcome break from tedium for an energetic naval officer forced to kick his heels at home between appointments.

Ordinarily, of course, a cutter's performance against the smugglers depended upon the character and reputation of her commander. We have seen in an earlier chapter that this sometimes left much to be desired. The Board of Customs' minute-books bear witness to a number of shameful episodes in which Revenue cutters slink off in the face of defiance from the more audacious of the smugglers. (It should be made clear at this point that such a charge was never levelled at a man-of-war employed in the Revenue service; the British tar struck his colours to no one, least of all a common smuggler.)

Revenue cutter *Greyhound* chasing.

In the 1770s a Captain Whitehead commanded the cutter *Eagle*, stationed on the north Yorkshire coast. In the course of a patrol off Saltburn one day, he fell in with a notorious contraband-runner, David Browning, known as 'Smoker'. When Whitehead hailed him, Smoker gave a dusty answer and called his men to quarters. As soon as the smuggler opened fire, Whitehead cravenly made off without putting the issue to the test.

This was Captain Whitehead's first brush with Browning, in which respect he was more fortunate than another somewhat unassertive cutter commander, Captain Mitchell of the *Swallow*. Smoker seemed to delight in making this officer's life a misery. Mitchell suffered several ignominious encounters with Smoker, culminating in a famous incident when the smuggler found *Swallow* resting at anchor in Salt-burn Bay, and after roundly abusing her commander, peremptorily ordered him to cut his cable and clear the anchorage, under pain of being sunk where he lay. Mitchell hastened to comply, making no attempt to do his duty and to effect Browning's arrest. Mitchell once complained petulantly that he 'seldom went for a cruise without being fired upon'. Small wonder, if he was such easy meat.

Browning's boat was a cutter of some 130 tons, well-armed and carrying upwards of forty men. She was a formidable adversary for any Revenue cruiser, but even so one cannot imagine Mr Pellew tolerating her presence for long in his territory. Smoker was eventually brought to book by HMS *Kite* cutter after a long chase down Channel from Beachy Head on 15 July 1788.

A frequent cause for disciplinary inquiry was the embezzlement of seizures, and particularly seizures of spirits, by cutter crews. There was a standing instruction to commanders that any seized goods were to be carried at the earliest opportunity to the nearest port and there lodged in the king's warehouse to await the Board's directions. The crews must have been greatly tempted when conveying a cargo of contraband spirits to take the chance of diverting a few tubs for their own comfort. Where the tubs were all accounted for, it was not difficult to 'bleed' one or two, and top up with water. Old letter-books reveal that the temptation was not always resisted.

Samuel Stokes, whose journal we have already looked into (see p 44), writes of his first capture in the *Rattlesnake* cutter:

> We sailed from Deptford the beginning of March 1809 to take our station in the Downs where we lay moor'd all the time I belonged to her. Our principal employment was to join the boats along shore to look out for smugglers. We took one after we had been very near three months, landing her cargo on the beach under the South Foreland, with seventy-two tubs of gineva and a great quantity of dry goods. This was the first prize I had been at the taking of since

I had been in the Revenue Service. I did not expect we should be allowed to make so free with the liquor, for we drank it out of the casks as it if had been small beer, until there was not a sober man in the three boat's crews except the chief mate.

There was little risk of detection here, presumably, as tubs did not hold a standard quantity and in any case were rarely filled to capacity.

One charge, made against two Cowes boatmen, reads, 'That in a seizure of 25 casks sent by them to the Custom House, three of them appear to have been pegged or spoiled [ie spiled] in several places and the liquor therein of very weak quality, also said casks were very deficient in quantity.' Their answer is worth quoting in full, but whether it gives a vivid picture of selfless devotion to duty and tenacious courage in the face of great odds or reveals a rare talent for colourful fiction, the reader must judge. Their superiors, we should add, were apparently satisfied with the explanation.

Answer of William Rant & George Granger

In the evening about seven o'clock, we made seizure of 35 casks at Luccomb. Immediately afterwards, [we] concluded to peg two casks with intent to know what we had seized, that we might in case of dispute ascertain what was in those casks.

At or near 10 o'clock the same night, six men came to us and demanded some of the liquor to drink. We refused them for some time, and at last a scuffle ensued and terminated in our favour. They immediately went away some small distance and returned each of them with a large stick. They swore they would have what liquor to drink they pleased, and also some of the tubs. Accordingly they laid hold of the two spoiled casks and began drinking.

After they had drinked as much as they pleased, they threw away the casks some distance, and swore if we made the least resistance in obstructing them in taking away what casks they thought proper, they would beat out our brains, the which we were obliged to submit to, having no arms to defend ourselves, and their numbers too many for us. They rescued ten casks after examining which were full and which were slack.

Directly after the six men were gone, we went and took up the two casks they had throwed away, which were almost leaked out owing to the spoil holes being undermost, and put them on the pile with the others remaining. We then consulted one with the other the readiest way to save the other goods, and concluded that it was the most expedient way to launch down the boat we had also seized for not being marked. The which we did, but with very great difficulty, she being very heavy and the surf running very high on the shore.

We had no sooner done this, put the kegs in the boat and got her off the shore, when the same people came down again with the same intent. We took to our oars, but owing to a contrary tide and wind at N.W. blowing fresh, did not reach our harbour till 5 o'clock the next morning, almost perished with cold, being wet to our middles all the night.

A tendency among the cutter crews to sample the goods was well known to the authorities; in fact the Board found it necessary to issue an instruction to cutter commanders to the effect that, after conveying goods to the king's warehouse, he and his mates were to search their

A matchlock musket of the pattern issued to the Waterguard.

own vessel for any which might have been kept back. As late as 1866 this order was still in force, for we find in the Coastguard Instructions for that year the commanders being reminded that whenever seizures were landed for delivery to the custom house, he and his mate together were to search diligently the boxes and bedding of the crew in case any of the contraband had been kept back. Those officers were warned that they would be held responsible if any of the goods were found to have been embezzled.

That the cutter crews should have been prone to pilfering from seizures (especially of spirits) was reprehensible, no doubt. But these were simple sailormen—albeit in revenue employment—in an age when sailors and spirituous liquor simply could not be kept apart, however sternly commanded. The temptations were many, but on the whole manfully resisted; seizures of spirits, after all, paid handsome rewards.

4

Smugglers' Devices

October. Fifty-eight tubs out of sixty, forming the cargo of the *Dove*, are crept off Downderry by the Looe boat.

July. Forty-one tubs are taken by the Cawsand crew in the galley *John*, of Cawsand; the remainder are still sunk off the Eddystone. They are part of a crop belonging to John ***, of Downderry, who was seen near Craft Hole, lying by a hedge drunk.

Coastguard log entries, Cawsand Station, 1833

After Bonaparte had been reduced at last and finally to dreaming of past glories on St Helena, the government was able to give more attention to domestic affairs. One of its most urgent tasks was the suppression of smuggling, which had risen to unprecedented heights. The Navy was made responsible for the organisation and manning of the greater part of the Revenue services; it now had men and ships to spare. On the other hand, the coming of peace re-opened the ports of Europe to the smugglers, as well as to honest traders; it also released, and no doubt returned to their former pursuits, the hundreds of smugglers who had been pressed into the Navy.

With the preventive force's increased strength and efficiency, the smuggling gangs soon learned that violence no longer paid, and were obliged to tread warily. We shall see that they were capable of great cunning and ingenuity, and the age-old conflict between smugglers and preventives assumed its modern guise—in the United Kingdom at any rate—of a battle of wits, rather than weapons.

With this post-war stepping-up of Revenue patrols both afloat and ashore, the free-traders ran a much greater risk of interception and of being caught red-handed with their goods. Their most usual cargo was spirits in tubs; it was also the bulkiest, and did not lend itself readily to concealment. It was necessary for the smuggling craft either to run itself on to an accessible beach to unload, or to lie offshore and transfer its cargo into 'tub-boats' for landing. Both methods took time and increased the risk of detection. The practice evolved of weighting the tubs with sinking-stones, dumping them overboard when approaching the shore, and leaving them attached to a recovery line, the end of which was buoyed on or close to the surface (see illustration below). This operation was known as 'sowing the crop'. It was not an entirely new departure, but whereas it had formerly been used only

Sketch of a sunken 'crop' of brandy or geneva tubs, showing the method of roping the tubs together and weighting them.

infrequently in areas where the preventives were particularly vigilant and determined, it now became a widespread practice.

Most smuggling craft were fitted with a wooden rail which ran the length of the hull inboard; this was known as the tub-rail. As the smuggler approached the shore, the tubs, already lashed to the sinking-rope and weighted with stones, were hung outside the hull ready for letting go. The sinking-rope was secured at intervals to the tub-rail with small lashings. Thus all that was necessary as the vessel ran over the chosen spot was to cut through the lashings, and the whole contrivance—tubs, sinking-rope and stones—fell clear. They could then be recovered at an opportune time.

Another ruse employed was to lash together a number of tubs in the form of a pyramid, designed to float low in the water and anchored to the sea-bed by a grapnel. The whole mass was painted sea-green, with the top few tubs painted white, and was almost impossible to distinguish in the surf. The 'crop' was recovered at leisure by small craft masquerading as inshore fishing-boats; it was concealed under their nets and landed when the coast was clear. H. N. Shore in *Smuggling Days and Smuggling Ways* recounts how one such 'fisherman' from Cawsand near Plymouth found himself in court with some searching questions to answer:

Q: You are an innkeeper and sailor, if I understand you rightly?
A: Yes.
Q: Is that all?
A: Mariner and innkeeper.
Q: Is that all the trades you follow?
A: Fishing sometimes.
Q: What do you fish for?
A: Different sorts of fish.
Q: Do you ever fish for half ankers?
A: Half-ankers?
Q: Casks of spirits—is that part of your fishing tackle?
A: No, I was never convicted of no such thing.
Q: I am not asking for that. You know what I mean. I am asking if it is part of your profession.
A: No, it was not.

Q: You never do such things?
A: What should I do it for?
Q: I cannot tell you. I ask whether you do it, not what you do it for.
A: I may choose to resolve whether I tell you or not.
Q: I will not press you if your conscience is tender. You will not tell me if you do a little stroke in the fair trade upon the coast. You will not answer me that question?
A: I am telling the truth.
Q: You will not answer?
A: No.
Q: Are you or are you not frequently in practice as a smuggler?
A: No!

One has the impression that this particular 'mariner and innkeeper' was more than a match for his inquisitor, whose questions do not reveal much expectation of a straight answer.

The Revenue officers were alert for any signs of crop-sowing. Preventive boats took to rowing off-shore in likely spots, towing a grapnel or 'creeping-iron' along the sea-bed, in the hope of catching up the sinking-rope. Sometimes, in rough weather, they were spared this task: the tubs were washed up high and dry on the adjacent beach as described in this letter to the Board (*Letter Book, port of Ipswich, 1756*):

> Honrs.—In the absence of the Collector, I beg to aquaint you that I have seized 45 gallons of brandy which were blown on shoare sunk by Smugglers and taken up by a Servant belonging to the Lord of the Manor at the sea side, and carried to the Custom House. The Surveyor also secured in the same manner about 6 hours after 36 gallons, and he understands the Lord of the Manor intends to lay a claim to it as Wrecked Goods, but they were in Prohibited Casks, and found with the slings upon them, and with part of the ropes by which sunk by, and a bag of stones for that purpose, and evry circumstance appearing so plain that they were concealed by Smugglers that we hope your Honrs. will please to grant an Order to condemn them for the Kings' use.
>
> Custom House
> Aldboro
> Robt Crabbe

The lord of the manor at this place was apparently one who enjoyed the ancient *droit* or right to impound any wreckage washed up on his foreshore: a right which generally belongs to the Crown. Contraband was, of course, an exception.

No smuggler was safe until his tubs were distributed among his clients. There was always the chance of encountering a preventive on the prowl. On 22 March 1817, a preventive boat patrolling the lower reaches of the river Orwell fell in with the *Daisy* yawl, which was heading up-river to Ipswich. The boat-sitter hailed her and with some difficulty prevailed upon her skipper to heave to and be boarded. As the boat-sitter swung over her bulwarks the skipper, Henry Palmer of Harwich, hastened to report that he had on board some tubs of spirits. There proved to be forty-eight of them, stowed below decks. Palmer claimed that he had caught them up in his nets whilst trawling and had every intention of handing them over to the proper authorities at the earliest opportunity. The boat-sitter was somewhat sceptical, and asked Palmer how it came about that, though he stated that he had had his nets out recently, they now appeared to be bone dry? And why were the tubs hidden below, rather than left in open view on deck? A thorough search of the vessel revealed a creeping-iron (not commonly an honest fisherman's tool of trade) the sand-burnished prongs of which indicated recent use. Evidence enough, felt the officer, and Palmer was in due course brought to trial and convicted, it being clear no doubt to the judge that he had reported his 'find' only when its discovery was imminent.

An ingenious variation on crop-sowing came to light near Dover in the 1820s. Half-ankers were encased in a thick, lumpy coating of plaster of Paris to disguise their distinctive shape and deposited under the famous white cliffs at the tide-line. Local people used to take carts on to the beach to collect lumps of chalk fallen from the cliff-face, for burning to make lime. Those who knew which lumps to look for had been taking home a very profitable cartload.

Sometimes a smuggler, with a cutter in hot pursuit and pressing close, would heave his cargo overboard tub by tub in an effort to distract his pursuers. This gambit was often successful; the cutter commander being torn between his natural instinct to secure the goods and his duty to catch the smuggler. Before long, commanders were given specific instructions for their guidance in such circumstances. It was emphasised, not for the first time, that the primary objective was to secure the persons of the smugglers. They were told (Instructions to Coastguard, 1832):

> When a smuggling vessel is chased, and the goods are thrown overboard, the chase is not to be given up to take possession of such goods, but the pursuit is to be continued whilst there is any possibility of coming up with and securing the vessel and crew; and in order that all chance of recovering the goods may not be lost, a 'Mark Buoy' is to be thrown overboard at such time as may appear most likely to lead to their discovery; observing that if the goods are floating, a buoy should be thrown amongst them, with a view to its drifting with them, and affording, in the event of their being found, a proof of their identity.

Positive identification of the goods concerned was important; indeed, it was vital to a successful prosecution. The Revenue officers needed to present a thoroughly cast-iron case in order to deny an opportunity to invariably sympathetic juries to acquit the smugglers.

A frequent plea made by the smugglers (or made on their behalf by sharp advocates, some of whom specialised in defending smuggling charges) was that they and their goods were wrongfully seized when they were outside the prescribed limits. Unless the cutter commander had been careful to precisely fix his position at the time of seizure such a claim was difficult to refute and often resulted in the offenders getting off. The commanders were instructed, therefore (Instructions to Coastguard, 1832):

> When a vessel is seized, or detained on suspicion, at sea, the Officer in command of the Cruizer or boat making the seizure is to take particular care that the soundings are immediately taken and that the distance from the shore at the precise time be clearly ascertained, by causing two points of land, or remarkable fixed objects on shore to be set, and the bearings thereof to be noted by two or more Officers, or persons well aquainted therewith, so that each of them may be able to swear to the bearings, to the course that the vessel was steering when first seen, and to her subsequent proceedings . . .

The regulations governing the licensing of small craft applied, broadly, to vessels of British nationality. British smugglers sought to evade these by acquiring foreign ship's papers and flying foreign colours. But few of them could speak the language of their 'adopted' country, and their performances when challenged were usually unconvincing. Some were ingenious enough to get themselves made burghers of Ostend, the Ostenders being willing to co-operate in a scheme which would benefit the profitable smuggling trade from their port. This expedient baffled the preventives for a time, until a ruling was obtained from the Attorney General that a British subject becoming a burgher of Ostend remained a British subject, with his vessel liable to forfeiture for any infringement of the law. Where the crews were mixed, English and French or Dutch, and a cutter encountered, the Englishmen would hide themselves away below decks, leaving their foreign shipmates to pass themselves off as honest sailors.

On 10 December 1819, the *Eagle* cutter was cruising off the south Kent coast in a snowstorm. At 8am she sighted through the swirling flakes a lugger under full sail, emerging from East Dungeness Bay and heading south-east. The *Eagle* approached to challenge her, whereupon the lugger hauled up closer to the wind, thereby increasing her speed. However, the *Eagle* gradually closed the gap until she was close enough to launch her eight-oared galley, under the command of the chief mate. The lugger, which was flying French colours, ignored the galley's repeated signals to stop, until the mate bellowed above the storm, 'If you don't heave-to, we'll fire right into you.' His meaning was clear enough, if not his words, and the Frenchman slacked away, allowing the Revenue men to board. The skipper answered Mr Gray's questions in French, stating that he was bound from Bordeaux to Calais—in which he was obviously lying, being miles out of his way. The crew was mustered and it was found that there were seven, not counting the skipper: five French and two English. These last two, claimed the skipper, were merely passengers; this in spite of the fact that their dress

—seaman's short jacket and canvas petticoat—proclaimed their calling clearly enough.

Unconvinced by protestations that there were no others aboard apart from these, the mate descended to the fore-peak, which was in total darkness, and prodded about him with his cutlass. A muffled yelp told him that he had made contact. 'Come on out', he ordered, and no fewer than seven bedraggled figures stumbled on deck. They were sent aft to join the others, and it was found that of the total crew, nine were English and five French. As a majority of the crew were English subjects, the lugger was seized and taken into port. (Under the law, if half or more of a boat's crew were subjects of the king, that boat was liable to seizure for any contravention regardless of the nationality claimed for the boat itself.) Although no contraband was found on board there was ample evidence—tub slings and hoops, and pieces of sinking-stones—that a cargo had recently been sunk off the Kent shore.

A curious incident is recorded in 1833. The Revenue cutter *Lively* was cruising off the Goodwins one Sunday morning in late October, when she sighted a suspicious craft, later identified as the yawl *Admiral Hood*. She gave chase. It was a long chase, during which the yawl jettisoned her cargo. The cutter disregarded the long line of tubs bobbing in the smuggler's wake and pressed the pursuit, eventually closing to within gun range. She opened fire: the smuggler hove to and was arrested.

During the subsequent trial at Ashford, a surprise witness for the defence came forward. He was Sir William Courtenay, a gentleman of some repute locally and a Member of Parliament for Canterbury. This worthy testified that he had witnessed the entire incident from a vantage point on the North Foreland. The Revenue men were lying, he said: he had seen the tubs floating there long before either craft appeared on the scene.

The Treasury lawyer conducting the prosecution was suspicious of this totally contradictory evidence and made some enquiries of his own. He was able to prove that Courtenay was attending divine service at a Herne Bay church at the material time. Courtenay was later arraigned for perjury and gaoled. No doubt he had good reasons for springing to the smugglers' defence, his somewhat shady past was probably known to them; but his perjury proved his undoing. His knighthood, it transpired, was as bogus as his evidence; he was later certified insane and incarcerated in an asylum.

It was not always necessary for a smuggler to cross to the Continent to load his wares. Many runs were made by small local craft which would leave harbour bound ostensibly for the fishing grounds, where they would rendezvous with a 'cooper'. A cooper was a foreign vessel (usually a Dutchman: the Dutch seemed to specialise in this, and still do) loaded with prohibited goods, which hovered outside the limits at a pre-determined place. Here it would transfer its cargo piecemeal into the boats. The latter would then return to harbour, possibly pausing en route to scoop up a few fish for the sake of appearances, with the contraband concealed under their gear. Thus they were never absent long enough to arouse suspicion.

A constant danger to the Revenue were the famous East Indiamen, which came up-Channel on the last leg of their long voyages, bound for London river. The officers and crews of these vessels would have laid in, during their travels, private stocks of high-duty goods such as silk, tobacco and tea. As the big merchantmen sailed along the south coast they were welcomed by hordes of small craft put out from shore, eager to bargain for these luxuries, and a brisk trade was carried on. The stately ships proceeded up to the Thames, shedding uncustomed goods on all sides. Their crews had no inhibitions about their illicit trading, and the Company turned a blind eye to the practice, even though it was presumably prejudicial to their own market to some extent. It seemed to be regarded as crew's 'perks'.

However, the Board was well aware of the situation and made sure that the cutter commanders were aware of it also. Each of them was instructed to accompany any East Indiaman through the extent of his station, and see him safely under the guard of the next cutter up-Channel before relinquishing his ward. If the suspect came to anchor en route the cutter was to hover nearby, stopping and searching any craft that put off from him. The commanders were sternly reminded of their duty to put a stop to 'the illicit practices that are continually committed' from the East Indiamen. Some commanders in the service of the Revenue endeavoured to shun these ships so avoiding having to attend them through their station. East Indiamen were to be boarded in the Downs by Customs officers who were to remain on board until the ship arrived at Gravesend.

The reluctance of some commanders to interfere was probably due to the fact that the well-armed East Indiamen had almost the status of men-at-war, and were at least as arrogant toward the preventives. Also, tailing a merchantman for 50 miles or so was a purely preventive function and not likely to be as profitable as capturing a loaded tub-boat or two.

This post-war period saw for the first time the widespread use of concealments in smuggling. The smuggler knew that he was as likely as not to encounter a Revenue patrol, and began to use his ingenuity a little more than hitherto. False bulkheads and keels, hollowed-out masts and spars became commonplace. Every conceivable method of concealment was utilised; once 30lb of plug tobacco was discovered in the hollow base of a ship's dog-kennel.

In December 1828 a boat belonging to the *Vigilant* cutter stopped and boarded off Birchington the *Alfred*, sprit-sail barge of London. Her skipper stated that he was bound from Arundel, coastwise to London, with a cargo of wood hoops. The *Vigilant's* men were evidently enthusiastic and skilful rummagers, for they found no fewer than 1,045 tubs of brandy and gin after they had cleared away the top 3ft of cargo, then dug through a deep layer of sand, and finally sawn through planking 2in thick.

That such contrivances were being used was well known to the authorities, and they made sure that the Revenue men were alive to the fact, as this instruction from a Board's general order dated 1822 shows:

> The Officers and Men are to use their best endeavours to detect the various schemes and devices adopted by smugglers to defraud the Revenue, particularly in the construction of concealments in coasters, colliers, and other traders, by means of false bottoms, false bulkheads, and other means; such vessels are to be vigilantly watched, particularly whilst discharging cargoes at places where there are no Officers or Men of the Customs present; and after their cargoes are discharged they should be carefully surveyed, and the depth and extent of their holds measured and examined with reference to their actual draught of water, length, breadth of beam, &c.

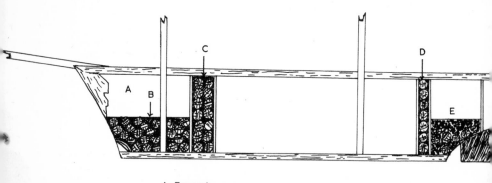

A Forepeak
B 21 Ankers concealed beneath forepeak
C 138 Ankers concealed in space formed by false bulkhead
D 188   "   "   "   "   "   "   "
E 26 Ankers concealed in bunk spaces in after crews' quarters

Typical concealments in hull construction; plan of the schooner *Good Intent* seized by Revenue cutter *Sylvia* in Mounts Bay on 14 March 1837.

When a special construction for the stowage of contraband was discovered, details of it were circulated to all ports. In this way staff were kept abreast of the latest trends. The following information was included in a general order dated 3 February 1823:

The Commissioners of Customs in London having transmitted to the Board the Copy of an Order issued to their Officers, from which it appears that the Tide Surveyor of the Port of Rye, upon examining the Smack *Hope* of that Port, burthen 21 24/94 Tons, discovered that she had false sides, forming a concealment which could hold from 80 to 100 Half Ankers, the Entrance to which was by Two Trap Hatches on each Side the Vessel, made to unship, as described in the Plan annexed . . .

The scope for constructions of this kind in old wooden vessels was enormous, especially for the stowage of non-bulky solids like tobacco, and great determination and zeal was called for on the part of the searchers. One vessel imported a cargo consisting of hundreds of poles of timber; a few of them were found to be hollowed out and stuffed with tobacco. The open ends of the poles had been made good very skilfully, and must have been most difficult to detect. Instances came to light of stowages for contraband which were quite inaccessible to the searchers from inboard; it was necessary for them to haul the vessel ashore and get at the space by cutting through the hull from outside.

As a measure of the sheer doggedness called for on the part of the men whose duty it was to find these concealments, we cannot do better than quote the report of a preventive officer stationed at Kilrush in Ireland in March 1822. It concerns a concealment discovered aboard the brig *Badajoz*, of London. This remarkable vessel was virtually a ship within a ship, with a space of eighteen inches or so all round for the stowage of contraband. The inner, false hull was complete in every detail, being fitted with the usual frames, ribs, and stringers.

It was at the head of one of these planks that I made the first attempt at discovery, and so confident were the crew of the vessel, that one of them handed a marline-spike and gave every assistance to explore the particular place, trusting that nothing would start the screws; and I am sure the heads of the planks were left without being nailed, that the minds of the persons searching might be the sooner satisfied, for so it was with persons that accompanied me. After prizing up the heads of the planks for an inch or two, the timbers and perfect vessel, as it were, showed themselves, and what was near satisfying my own mind, was natural decay in the side of one of the planks, which I found afterwards to be also intended for deception. Three times did we come and leave this place, satisfied that all was correct there, until, wearied from searching, I made the last attempt at the same place, and succeeded in forcing one of the planks out of its berth. My suspicious were immediately aroused by the dryness and huskiness of the lower planks and screws, never having seen even a copper-bottomed vessel that did not show an oozing of some kind through the outside plank, I therefore persevered and got the next plank forced out of its place, and the screw holes shortly led to a trap-scuttle and the concealment. In the sides of the forecastle berths were openings exactly on the same principle as that described, but it was not till after the concealment was emptied that the other traps were discovered from the inside, so completely concealed were the whole, which a person knowing the secret would have unravelled in a minute or two. There was no boy on board, for fear he should disclose the secret.

The smugglers' painstaking ingenuity knew no bounds. A craft bearing the quaint name *Wig Box* and belonging to one John Punnet of Folkestone was seized there in 1822 by a midshipman of the coast blockade. His men had discovered six gallons of spirits, sloshing about inside her three oars, two masts, bowsprit and bumpkin. Punnet had hollowed out these fittings and lined them with tin. One feels that he deserved to get away with his comparatively modest cache: he had no doubt done so on many previous occasions before his luck ran out.

By the 1820s, however, such elaborate subterfuges were only just coming into vogue; the bulk of contraband was still being landed on open beaches, or sunk offshore. One of the anti-smuggling laws made it a penalty, under pain of six months' imprisonment, to signal from the beach or cliffs to craft out at sea. (It remains an offence to the present day.) Nevertheless, such signalling went on all the time; it was necessary for the smugglers to know that the preventives were not about before running the goods, and that the shore gang were ready and waiting. Of course, there was a risk that the flashing light would also alert Revenue craft in the vicinity, or patrols ashore, as happened in the case of Galton and Ellis, according to a magistrates' court record at Poole, Dorset, 1818:

The information of Joseph Carter, Sitter of His Majesty's Customs and belonging to the Preventive Boat at Swanage.

On June 16 Carter was on duty at midnight at Haven House near Studland. Having seen a suspicious light there he hid beneath some seaweed on the shore and saw two men—John Galton and Timothy Ellis—putting tubs of liquor into a boat at the quay. A third person ran off. Galton and Ellis were taken to the Custom House at Poole and Lodged in the watch-house. They were later conveyed to Swanage, impressed, and transferred to an Algerine sloop.

Carter, when he 'hid beneath some seaweed' was employing a well-established ruse of the preventive men. Its invention has been credited to one Richard Newman, a Riding Officer based at Christchurch at the close of the eighteenth century. When this officer, expecting a run to be made, had a detachment of dragoons at his disposal he would instruct them to dig 'graves' for themselves in the sand at the likely landing place. The soldiers, with their firearms primed, would lie prone in the shallow trenches to be covered with sand by their comrades, only their heads being left exposed. Their heads were then crowned with a mantle of seaweed. The unsuspecting smugglers would run their boat up the beach and begin to unload the contraband. At a pre-arranged signal the very earth would sprout armed soldiery, as if sown with dragon's teeth.

It is not surprising that duties in aid of the Revenue were not popular with the soldiers. They were eligible for a share in the reward for a seizure, but in most regiments such payments were appropriated to regimental funds, and the men themselves saw little benefit—certainly not enough to compensate them for the labour of cleaning uniform and equipment after a night spent buried in damp sand.

Sometimes signalling from the shore would be by means of a light flashed from inside the mouth of a cave, or by using a specially designed lantern so that the signal could be seen only from seawards. E. Keble Chatterton, a Customs historian, lists the following means of signalling used by smugglers:

1. The commonest signal at night was to wave a lantern from a hill or some prominent landmark, or from a house suitably situated.

Smugglers' Devices

2. To take a flint and steel and set fire to a bundle of straw near the edge of a cliff.
3. To burn a blue light.
4. To fire a pistol.
5. The above were all night-signals, but for day-work the craft could signal to the shore or other craft by lowering and raising a certain sail so many times.

It is surprising to see numbers 3 and 4 in this list as they were the signals most often employed by the preventives. One would have thought that their use would have brought quite the wrong response, as far as the smugglers were concerned.

A modern Waterguard rummage crew at work.

Every fresh device resorted to by the smugglers sooner or later became known to the Revenue men. The new centralised organisation ensured that such intelligence was passed to all stations expeditiously, and a real effort was made to keep one jump ahead of the smugglers, to the great benefit of the Revenue.

5

East and West

. . . A Gang of Smugglers who have so many years Triumphed over the Officers of the Revenue and struck Terrour into the Country for so many years.

Letter from Surveyor of Kent Riding Officers to the Board's Solicitor 1747

Smuggling in Britain, for obvious geographical reasons, was concentrated on (though by no means confined to) the southern coast. It should not be assumed, however, that the smugglers of, say, Essex and Dorset had anything in common, apart from their detestation not so much of the Revenue laws (the evasion of which gave them a fat living) as of the agents of the Revenue who sought to enforce them.

Such factors as local demand for their goods, distance from the nearest Continental ports at which contraband could be loaded, the strength of preventive forces in their locality and many others, determined the *modus operandi* of the smugglers in a particular area. Dissimilarities of temperament and moral tone between the men of the East and the men of the West there may have been—but these are deep waters into which the author is not inclined to venture. Sufficient to say that methods did vary and this is an opportune point at which to

76

mark the differences between the smuggling fraternity in two distinct areas, namely, Devon and Cornwall on the one hand, and the south-east coast of England on the other.

Kent

Of all the fair counties which girdle the sceptred isle of Britain, there can be little doubt that first prize for smuggling must go to Kent: since the days of the wool-owlers it had been a way of life.

Romney Marsh—that strange, brooding wedge of desolation with Dungeness at its point, jutting into the Channel—beautiful in its own way under summer skies and dotted with fat Romney sheep, but in the long winter months lashed by Channel gales, abandoned to the sad cry of the curlew, its dark landscape the haunt of ghosts and other night walkers. What better place for the smugglers to ply their trade? Remote, insular, lone beaches for their landings and flat terrain for their pack horses; scattered hamlets whose cowed inhabitants preferred *not* to see the gentlemen ride by. The locals were well looked after so long as they behaved themselves; a tub of brandy perhaps, rolled into an overgrown corner of the churchyard to await collection later, or dropped off at the inn. Revenue officers who passed that way did so at their peril unless in numbers and well armed, when their progress and intentions were mysteriously known ahead of them all along their route.

Reference has already been made to the smugglers who infested the countryside in gangs; a law unto themselves, prepared to give battle to any Revenue force bold enough to hinder them and also to any rival gang which might covet their wares. Romney Marsh had more than its share of them. The local populace—small traders, innkeepers, farmers and their hired hands, fishermen—none of them had any liking for the Customs law or its agents. They looked upon the smugglers as benefactors: their champions against oppressive taxation.

Unfortunately, like many champions of the people before and since, smuggling gangs soon grew arrogant; as contemptuous of those not of their number as of the Revenue. The most notorious of these armed mobs was the 'Hawkhurst Gang'. They took their name from the pleasant hamlet just over the Kent/Sussex border and some ten miles inland, which they had made their base. The Hawkhurst Gang roamed far and wide in their illicit activities; west to the coast of Dorset and east to the Kentish Knock, but their favourite territory was Romney Marsh, where they held undisputed sway for many years. The other gangs were as terrified of them as were the local residents, and kept well out of their way. During their ascendancy they perpetrated many murders, including the brutal slaying of an unarmed Customs officer (see p 82).

The local Revenue officers were far from convinced that Kentish magistrates were doing their duty without fear or favour; they suspected, justifiably perhaps, that those worthies were in collusion with, or in dread of, the smugglers. Without backing from the courts, and with their own inadequate resources, many Customs men like the writer of this letter, must often have been close to despair (Board of Customs Letter Book, port of Rochester, 1740).

We are very much infested with Smugglers that go in such large Bodies armed with Blunderbusses and other ofencive Weapons, severall of which have called at my House, swaring they would kill me or any other Officer they should meet with. About a fortnight past we had an excise Officer shot at Plackstead, within five miles of Tunbridge, by 16 or 17 men armed as aforesaid, and last Wensday the Excise Officer of Seven Oaks was taken Prisoner by uperwards of 20 Smuglers, who beat him and Caried him to the Bull head at Sprats Bottom near Farnborow, ware they unloaded their goods, kept him all night till they loaded again, and went clear of, and last night Mr Griffin, Supervisor of Excise, was going his servay with the Excise Officer of Tunbridge, was Beat and Cutt in so Violent a manner that his life is Dispard of by a Large Parcell of Smuglers within a mile of Tunbridge. They likweise Beat and Missuses severall Private People in the road, making them kneel down in the mud and beg their Pardons. Sir I Humbly Beg your utmost Endevours we may be suply'd with some Soldiers.

The Hawkhurst Gang breaking into the Custom House at Poole.

The plain fact was that there was no law in the land, no police force in the mid-eighteenth century to enforce law and order; local magistrates simply dared not attempt to do their duty in upholding the king's peace. The preventive officers were powerless against the gangs and were plainly seen to be so by the local populace.

The Hawkhurst Gang, just referred to, were notorious for their peculiar brutality; they had a predilection for flogging, and most of their victims were beaten to death. This gang's most infamous exploit occurred in February 1748. A couple of months previously, a large contraband cargo of tea and brandy, the smugglers' chief stock-in-trade, had been seized by the Revenue cutter *Swift* when about to be landed on a beach near Boscombe. The news of this disaster was conveyed to Thomas Kingsmill, leader of the Hawkhurst Gang, together with the information that the goods were lodged in the king's warehouse on Poole quay. He and his men were audacious enough to stage a carefully planned night attack on Poole Custom House and rescue the goods.

What business had Kingsmill and his mob so far from their native heath? An illuminating statement was made by a witness at Kingsmill's trial, when he was eventually brought to justice in May 1749. The witness, a Dorset man, described how he and his fellows, considering the Custom House to be too well guarded to allow of success, were for abandoning the venture. Kingsmill would have none of this, and made it plain that he would go ahead, whatever the opposition, 'We call them the east country people', said the witness; 'they were fetched to break open the Custom House' (Russell Oakley, *The Smugglers of Christchurch*). Such was Kingsmill's reputation as a desperado among the smugglers along the entire coast.

News of this daring attack spread far and wide, and as the smugglers made their way inland with the booty they were cheered on by admiring rustics at the roadside. Among the onlookers, Daniel Chater, a shoemaker of Fordingbridge, recognised one of the smugglers—an old acquaintance named John Diamond, alias 'Dimer', and called to him. Diamond returned his greeting and as he rode by, tossed a bag of tea at Chater's feet.

When news of the outrage reached the Board in London, they immediately caused reward notices to be distributed throughout the south and south-west, offering handsome sums for information leading to the arrest of the gang members. Such notices were often circulated, without much optimism; results were rarely forthcoming. However, Chater decided for one reason or another to lay information against his benefactor, and Diamond was soon after apprehended.

The Board's solicitor needed Chater's testimony in order to secure a conviction, and accordingly a Riding Officer, William Galley, was despatched to Fordingbridge to escort Chater to Chichester, venue of the trial. Galley duly met up with his charge and the pair of them set off for Chichester early on the morning of Sunday, 14 February 1748.

Neither of them was seen again alive. After several days had passed and the two men failed to appear, the Board, thoroughly alarmed and fearing the worst, stirred themselves and instructed the Collector at Southampton to find out what he could. Eventually a horrifying story was unfolded.

The two men, weary at the end of the day's ride, had fetched up at a small wayside inn. Galley was travelling incognito of course, but the innkeeper, in common with many of his calling, was closely involved with the smugglers and shared their ability to smell a preventive man a mile off. Galley, relaxed after his long day on the road, expansive under the influence of the refreshment with which his friendly host plied him and his travelling-companion, was unwise enough to divulge the purpose of his journey. Within an hour the innkeeper had got word of his guests and their business to six members of the Hawkhurst Gang who lived locally.

Galley and Chater retired to bed, blissfully unaware that in a small room just below them, in the light of a guttering candle, their fate was being decided. Three of the gang, William Steel, William Carter and William Jackson, were for cutting their throats and dumping them in a deep well at the back of the inn-yard. The innkeeper, not unnaturally, objected to this, and favoured getting them down to the beach for shipment to France; all were unanimous that Chater's dangerous testimony should never be heard at Chichester. It seems likely that they were still undecided when the meeting broke up. While the innkeeper made ready their horses, the smugglers burst into the room occupied by Galley and Chater, hauled them from their beds, bound them hand and foot, and dragged them downstairs and out into the stable-yard beating them mercilessly. They were lifted on to a horse, and set facing each other, with their hands bound and their feet lashed under the horse's belly. They were then led away, the smugglers walking alongside and beating the unfortunate pair with whips and cudgels until their arms tired, when they were relieved by eager companions. At one point Galley, slumped senseless, fell beneath the horse's belly and was dragged along in that position for half a mile or so before being roughly hauled upright. At length the gang, tiring of their sport, reined the horses and threw their victims to the ground. Galley was obviously close to death; he was bleeding from the nose and mouth, and, still breathing, he was dragged off the road into a field and buried alive. His body was found months later. Chater lingered a little longer; after more beatings he was thrown into a dry well. The murderers then dropped large stones down the well until his groans could no longer be heard.

When the news of this barbaric deed—brutal and bestial even by the standards of the much-romanticised free-traders—leaked out, a general hue and cry was set up. One by one the murderers were tracked down. They were arraigned for trial at Chichester in January 1749, condemned and executed and their bodies hung in chains. It is certain that the well-merited end of those six bully-boys did not call forth many tears from the local citizenry; the gangs were getting altogether too big for their boots.

Part of the trouble had been that in 1745 the Customs duties on a number of commodities, including tea and spirits, were drastically cut (temporarily, as it transpired) and so were the smugglers' profits. The gangs began to look elsewhere for easy pickings. Well-organised, well-armed, and without fear of the law, they began to terrorise the countryside, robbing and looting as they pleased. Many Romney farmers were robbed of their wool-fells when the gangs took to 'owling' again, and had to stand by helpless as their stocks of fodder were raided for the smugglers' horses. The Hawkhurst Gang were always well to the fore in these activities, and for a long time no one dared to stand against them. But eventually Kingsmill and his mob met their match.

It happened at the village of Goudhurst, close to the Sussex border and some six miles from the Gang's headquarters. The Hawkhurst

The murder of Galley and Chater; nineteenth-century etching by 'Phiz'.

Gang had for some time preyed mercilessly on the villagers—as they were neighbours there was perhaps some extra cause for animosity. The time came, however, when the Goudhurst men would take no more. Under the leadership of one of their number who was lately returned from the wars, they formed themselves into a kind of militia. Arming themselves as best they could, they drilled conscientiously and practised with the few muskets and blunderbusses available. Kingsmill got news of this activity and waylaying one of the villagers, forced him to divulge their preparations. The smugglers' chief was enraged by the challenge to his authority and determined to teach the yokels a lesson. He released his captive, with a promise to the villagers that his gang would attack on a stated day, and that no house would be left standing in Goudhurst and no man left alive.

Kingsmill had sadly underrated the mettle of the Goudhurst men. Having, in his arrogance, forewarned them of the attack (they knew he had no choice but to make good his boast) they made their preparations.

True to his promise, on the appointed day Kingsmill led his men toward the village. The villagers were ready and waiting. With the churchyard as their headquarters they had stationed their marksmen in barns, lofts, and other vantage points on the approach road. When the smugglers eventually appeared, milling in the roadway and shouting dire threats, a volley of musket fire stopped them in their tracks. They ran for cover, leaving three of their number dead on the road. Nonplussed, but unable to believe that here were ordinary citizens determined and resolute enough to meet force with force, they re-formed and stormed into the village. They met with no tangible resistance, and the women and children had been evacuated long before, but as they stormed through the village street, roaring vengeance, one by one they were felled by musket fire, directed from rooftops, the church tower, from behind walls and doorways. Having lost a third of their number in this fashion, the gang's bravado deserted

84

them and they fled, taking their wounded with them. Goudhurst was troubled no more.

Goudhurst's signal victory over the gangsters was unique, however; it is the only recorded instance where local citizens got together in an organised way to offer defiance to their oppressors. The Hawkhurst Gang, despite their humiliating setback at the hands of the Goudhurst men, continued their depredations for a little longer; it seems that other harassed communities were not inspired by Goudhurst's valorous example. Their final break-up began after the murders of Galley and Chater and the executions which followed. In the general odium following the trial, and the public recounting of the horrific details, some of the gang—to save their own skins—laid information against their fellows. One by one they were gathered in, including Kingsmill, their leader. He and several others were convicted of breaking into the Poole Custom House and all were hanged. The Hawkhurst Gang ceased to exist.

Other smuggling gangs continued active in Kent for the next hundred years or so. Two of the best known were the North Kent Gang whose base of operations was the Whitstable/Herne Bay area, and the Aldington Gang, named after the village on the north-eastern fringe of Romney Marsh, some four miles inland from Hythe. But their activities took place at a later date, and are proper to a later chapter (see pp 95–7).

Devon and Cornwall

The story of smuggling activity in Devon and Cornwall presents a contrast to that of Kent and Sussex, not merely because the volume of illicit trade carried on in the West Country was so much greater per head of population than elsewhere in England, but because the nature of the trade itself presented different problems to the smuggler and the Revenue alike.

The Cornishmen were every bit as devoted to the pursuit of free-trade as their brethren in the south-east, but went about it in a different way. It was notable that they rarely resorted to armed force (at least, not on the same scale as elsewhere), preferring to use guile in achieving their ends.

It was the Westcountryman's native ingenuity which gave birth to the quite brilliant idea of crop-sowing—that and his intimate knowledge of tides, currents and weather in his locality. He was as familiar with the convolutions of the sea-bed in his area as with the outline of the coomb beside his cottage. Above all he was a seaman. His necessarily long sea crossing to load his goods meant that the voyage itself was the major part of the entire enterprise. The lander was a figure almost unknown in the West Country; usually the smuggler there owned his boat or boats, risked his own capital and distributed his own wares.

The Cornish smugglers had many advantages. Given their much indented coastline with its barren, thinly-populated hinterland, plus the comparative paucity of waterguard patrols, they had a good chance of making their runs undetected if their luck held as far as the chosen beach. To that extent their task was easier. But the risk involved in the actual crossing was perforce much greater than that accepted by the men of Kent and Sussex, with their short hauls across the neck of the Channel to the near Continental ports.

The Westcountry smuggler did his 'shopping' in the Channel Islands or in ports on the coast of Brittany. Throughout the eighteenth century and well into the nineteenth, the Channel Islands, and Guernsey in particular, were an entrepot for contraband goods. By 1750, virtually the entire economy of the island was built upon the transhipment and warehousing of goods destined for the holds of smuggling craft from the south of England.

By ancient charter, Guernsey was exempted from Excise and Customs levies; neither was she bound by the various anti-smuggling statutes in force on the mainland. Lying snug in harbours where the Revenue writ did not run, the smugglers loaded their illicit cargoes into their illegal craft, sometimes masquerading under false colours and *noms de guerre* as a precaution against Customs spies.

This happy state of affairs was allowed to continue unchecked until 1767, when the British government established a Custom House at St Peter Port and stationed two revenue cutters there. Their commanders were ordered to ensure that 'no brandies or spirits be imported into or exported from these islands in casks of less than sixty gallons, or in vessels under fifty tons burden'. These regulations were already being enforced on the mainland as part of the legislative armoury against the 'free-traders'. Smugglers in general, and Cornishmen in particular, favoured small fast vessels (many of them being open boats —long galleys propelled by twelve or more oars), and contraband spirits were usually carried in 'ankers' and 'half-ankers', small tubs which could be easily handled and transported.

Such unwonted interference on the part of the central government was not taken too seriously in Guernsey, nor did it continue for long; the cutters were soon withdrawn to perform a more pressing naval function. It was not until 1805, and in the face of much protest from the islanders, that Guernsey and her sister islands were drawn into the ambit of the Customs law by Act of Parliament.

The arguments deployed by the Royal Courts of Guernsey in support of their immunity were somewhat ingenious. In September 1800, in reply to a Crown Commissioner, they indignantly denied encouraging the trade and then continued in a long and rambling plea, that firstly, smuggling is an intolerable evil not to be countenanced at any price; secondly, since it cannot be prevented, it is better that any profit accruing should go to the king's loyal subjects of Guernsey, rather than to his sworn enemy across the Channel: thirdly, although a tiny minority of the generally amiable smuggling fraternity are depraved enough to offer armed resistance to His Majesty's officers acting in pursuit of their lawful duty, they could do so with greater facility were they based elsewhere.

The prosperous merchants of Guernsey referred in their petition to the plight of the Cornish tin miners (the smugglers' best customers) who, they claimed, would languish for want of a dram. Those unfortunates 'mostly live underground, to whom spirits are beneficial, but who, nevertheless, could not afford to pay for entered spirits'. Surely human compassion can go no further!

Nevertheless, there was no denying that the French, ever ready to exploit any situation which could embarrass her ancient enemy, were anxious that the English smugglers should be given every encouragement. The bulk of the trade did shift as the Guernsey men predicted that it would, to French ports, and to Roscoff in particular. The great Bonaparte himself said of the smugglers, after his final defeat:

> They did great mischief to your Government; they took from France annually forty or fifty millions [francs-worth] of silks and brandy. During the war they had a part of Dunkirk allotted to them, to which they were restricted; but as they latterly went out of their limits, committed riots, and insulted everybody, I ordered Gravelines to be prepared for their reception, where they had a little camp for their accommodation.

It was evidently too much to ask of any true-born Englishman, even an outlawed smuggler, to refrain from offering affront to a Frenchman whenever the opportunity presented itself. It is difficult to believe that this little enclave of sturdy Francophobes did more good than harm to the French cause, in spite of the retrospective wishful thinking of the ex-Emperor. Few of the Westcountrymen actually transferred their domicile to France and those who did were fugitives from justice who had good reason not to spend longer on their native soil than they could help, as their presence in the area would soon become known to the authorities.

Some small communities on the coasts of Devon and Cornwall, villages such as Cawsand, Looe and Polperro, subsisted largely on the proceeds of smuggling. An officer of the Coastguard compiled a list of no fewer than fifty-two boats and eighty-one men belonging to the tiny fishing village of Cawsand actively employed in smuggling during the decade 1832–42. By this date they were probably small open boats, and their owners fishermen who did a little smuggling on the side.

Earlier, in an official return dated 20 January 1785, of *armed* smuggling craft plying on the coast of Cornwall, the following were listed:

Stag   Lugger, 90 tons, 30 men, all equipped with side-arms

Happy-go-Lucky Lugger, 80 tons, 35 men, all with sidearms

Happy-go-Lucky Cutter, 100 tons, 14 guns, 30 men

Glory   Shallop (ie sloop), 70 tons, 20 men, all with side-arms

Sweepstakes   Lugger, 250 tons, 26 guns (12 and 9-pounders) 60 men, numerous boats 30–46ft long with 6–12 oars

In addition to these there were innumerable smaller boats engaged in the trade.

Consider the last-named in the list. The *Sweepstakes* must have been more than a match for any revenue cutter in service at that time, except for some of the men-of-war employed. The biggest revenue cutter in commission at that date was the *Repulse*, 210 tons, with a complement of 33 and mounting 22 guns; she was stationed at Colchester. Most of the cutters were a good deal smaller and less well armed.

Lieutenant the Honourable H. N. Shore, RN (later Lord Teignmouth) held an appointment as a Coastguard Divisional Officer at Fowey in the eighteen-seventies. This officer took a lively interest in his profession and is the author of many works on old-time smugglers. In particular, he did a good deal of historical research into smuggling activity in the neighbourhood of Fowey during the hey-day of the free-traders and was able to interview old men who in their youth had taken part in runs from Roscoff and elsewhere. From them he gathered many verbatim accounts of those eventful times—with some extra colour added, no doubt, as is usually the way when old gentlemen reminisce, but the stories are no less worth repeating for that.

There were the hazards of the long crossing in the bitter and treacherous mid-winter:

> Twas bitter work of a winter time—that crossing from Rusco [Roscoff] and Cherbourg—sleet and snow, and blow, blow, blow, fit to tear your hair off. By gosh, if I was to tell the young chaps nowadays what I've been through they wouldn't believe me. They seem a different breed, to my mind, to the chaps of sixty or seventy years back [where have we heard that before?] they ain't got the go in 'em for that smuggling business, not now.

A noted local smuggler was drowned, together with his crew, during just such a crossing:

> That's true what you say about poor Phil Kingcup being lost. I was coming back from Cherbourg the same night; werry stormy, it was, though I've seen it wuss, still there was the douce of a kick-up of sea. We was going to start together; but when we got under weigh Phil sung out they would'nt be ready for another half-hour—had to get their tops'l down and stowed. However, after a bit, we'd see'd 'em following, and that was the last was ever seed of the boat under sail. Next that was heard of her was when she drifted on shore, with all her tubs hung round her, and the ballast gone, by Hope Cove. The bodies—four of 'em—was seen lying on the bottom in deep water, just outside. I saw them mysel'; 'twas the strangest sight I ever see'd, for you could tell their faces as they lay on the bottom, it was that clear.

There were humorous incidents as well as tragic:

> Old Sammy Sell of Polruan arranged with some parties around Fowey to fetch a cargo of tubs—300, I think—from Rusco, and run them in Fowey Harbour. He got over to the French coast right enough, and just off Rusco fell in with the *Susannah*, a dandy-rigged cruiser [see glossary], what belonged to the Cossand [Cawsand] Coastguard station. She was a smuggler fust going off; and had been captured by the Cossand crew some years before, and then handed over to Mr. Foote, Chief Officer there, as a cruiser. She had tanned sails—same as she carried when a smuggler. Well, as soon as the *John* got near the *Susannah* someone on board the cruiser hailed and asked old Sammy where he was bound to, and Sammy, thinking she was a Cawsand smuggling boat, answered back, 'Same place as you'. Well, the *Susannah* didn't stop her, 'twouldn't have been any good, as she had no tubs in her then, and when

Sammy got into Roscoff he found a lot more Cawsand boats there waiting for their cargoes; and the chaps aboard asked him if he had fellen in with any boats outside, and he said ,'Oh, yes; we were hailed by a craft and asked where we were bound', and when he described the craft, the Cawsand men said, 'Why, that's the *Susannah* !' Well, old Sammy was that scared, he took nothing in but just sailed right back home again to Plymouth, and got safe in without even being boarded by the Coastguards. Sammy never went smuggling again after that.

H. N. Shore quotes an anonymous Customs informer, resident in Roscoff, who sent regular returns of smuggling craft frequenting the port, together with details of their cargoes. Here is his list of departures for 15–27 March 1833:

Goldfinch	with 90 tubs for Plymouth			
Four Brothers	,,	20	,,	,, ,,
Supply	,,	60	,,	,, Dartmouth
Rose	,,	80	,,	,, The Lizard
Goldfinch	,,	120	,,	,, Dartmouth (2nd trip)
Eagle	,,	150	,,	,, Fowey
Love	,,	125	,,	,, Coverack
William	,,	80	,,	,, Falmouth

Assuming this to be a typical list for the winter months, and that the 'tubs' are half-ankers of four gallons capacity, we may form some conception of the quantity of contraband spirits entering Cornwall and Devon alone, in the course of a year.

Not all these cargoes reached the consumer; some were jettisoned in the course of a stormy crossing, when it came to a case of saving a labouring vessel and the lives of those in her—though as may be imagined, this was a desperate measure taken only as a last resort. Others fell prey to prowling revenue cutters, or were recovered from the sea-bed by the 'creeping-irons' of Waterguard boats. But the profits on a successful run were vast, more than enough to cover some losses; indeed, the smugglers were said to be generally content if they got one cargo through out of three.

The smuggling trade in the West Country, as elsewhere, went into a rapid decline in the mid-1800s. The reason was purely and simply an economic one—tariffs were greatly reduced. The smugglers' profits were just not worth the risk any more.

Curiously, this diminution in Cornish lawlessness has been attributed to the spread of Methodism there. John Wesley himself claimed as early as 1763 that 'the detestable practice of cheating the King is no more found in our societies' (ie the new congregations). At that date, of course, smuggling had barely begun to get into its stride.

Wesley began his evangelical crusade in Cornwall in 1743. He preached there intermittently for fifty years, and to some effect. He could certainly claim to have put the moralistic skids under the other great Cornish vice of wrecking, which did virtually die out during his ministry. It may be that he was confusing the lesser sin with the greater.

The Anglican clergy, at least, suffered no theological misgivings

Smugglers bringing goods up from the beach.

when it came to free-trading; the parson has always figured largely in smuggling lore. Indeed, many Westcountry smugglers were exceedingly pious men. One such was Captain Henry Carter, of Penzance. He had a forceful personality and a penchant for preaching. During a long exile in Roscoff he was in the habit, on Sabbath mornings, of rounding up the more tractable of the English smuggling community there and inflicting a service on them. 'The men took off their hats', he records with satisfaction, 'all very serious, no laffing, no trifling conversations'. (See under Carter, bibliography.)

But few of those stout souls, Methodist or not, would concede that the Almighty was on the side of the Revenue, and the Westcountrymen persisted in their waywardness for as long as it paid well.

6

Blockaders and Coastguard

The Comptroller-General directs that officers and men be publicly informed that a list will in future be kept of every person serving at a station within which a run took place, and that no such officer or man will be considered eligible for promotion or entitled to any mark of indulgence or favour.

General Order to Coastguard, 1829

Once Napoleon was defeated, more men-of-war were made available to supplement and stiffen the Revenue fleet. We have seen that naval officers were appointed to command many of the cutters. Another measure taken by the Navy at the government's behest was the establishment, in 1817, of the coast blockade.

The blockade was originally confined to the coasts of Kent and Sussex. Two men-of-war were stationed offshore; one in the Downs, the other at Newhaven, to act as base or headquarters ships. Their crews were landed, split up into small detachments in charge of a petty officer and posted to the several Martello towers strung along that coast. The coastline was divided into 'blockade stations', each of which was commanded by a lieutenant of the Royal Navy. The men patrolled the shore adjacent to their towers, on the lookout for smuggling activity.

The idea was sound; it was the concept of the coast blockade which, in the main, led to the birth of the Coastguard service a few years later, virtually the same system extended to cover the entire seaboard. In practice the blockade was not as effective as it should have been. It was not a popular assignment among the seamen of the fleet, and tended to attract the worst types from the lower deck. Isolated in small groups as they were, without close supervision, discipline was lax. Boredom and lack of active employment led to much drunkeness; before long many of the men had been corrupted by the smugglers and were working hand-in-glove with them. The blockade was continued, however, until 1831 when its functions were transferred to the Coastguard.

The men of the blockade were, generally speaking, as desperate a crowd of cut-throats as any smuggling gang, albeit under naval discipline. If for no other reason, they were the ideal force to set against the gangs.

The blockade was commanded by Captain J. M. McCulloch, RN, known in the Navy, with good reason, as 'Flogging Joey'. He was well aware that he had the dregs of the fleet under his command, but he was a born leader who understood his men. McCulloch determined to obliterate the smuggling gangs in his area.

His first success was with the North Kent Gang. In October 1821 the North Kent Gang ran a cargo ashore on the beach near Reculver. A coast blockade mishipman, with four men, boldly ran in among the smugglers; they discharged their pistols to some effect and laid about them with cutlasses; the smugglers dropped their loads and fled. In the *mêlée* one of the smugglers was recognised by the blockaders; he was later arrested and persuaded to lay information against the others. Armed with the man's testimony a Bow Street runner named (believe it or not!) James Bond, was despatched from London to effect the arrest and prosecution of the rest of the gang.

Bond successfully prosecuted all the members of the gang who had taken part in the run. Most of them were sentenced to transportation for life; four of the leaders were condemned to death and publicly hanged on Penenden Heath. So, after many lawless years and with the killing or wounding of many Customs officers to their score, the North Kent Gang was effectively obliterated. 'Flogging Joey' now turned his baleful eye upon the Aldington smugglers, rivals to the North Kent men.

By 1820 the Aldington Gang (referred to earlier, p 85) had become well established and had already made several runs in south Kent. In November of that year they had landed a huge cargo of spirits at Shorncliffe, when no fewer than 300 of the gang were present at the scene. They were organised in the usual manner, half the party acting as porters to bring the tubs up from the beach and 'batsmen' deployed on either side, covering the landing. A small naval force from the nearby Sandgate watch-house courageously sallied out under the command of a midshipman, but were soon repulsed.

With the North Kent men out of the way, McCulloch determined that the Aldington Gang should not get a moment's respite from Revenue attention; that they should never again run a cargo without blockade intervention and determined pursuit. This policy was resolutely followed for the next four years or so; the smugglers were continually harassed and dared not operate without a heavily-armed fighting party of a hundred or more. No spectacular successes were achieved during this period by the blockade and few arrests were made; indeed, Captain McCulloch's men suffered many casualties, outnumbered as they were. But there can be no doubt that the smugglers' activities were greatly curtailed as a result of such tenacious opposition.

The Aldington Gang eventually met their Nemesis in the form of another Bow Street runner, George Ruthven—famous for his arrest of the Cato Street conspirators in 1820. Ruthven and his colleagues were aided no doubt by the awesome reputation which those renowned 'Robin Redbreasts' (their only uniform was a scarlet waistcoat) had gained by their fearless and impartial pursuit of wrongdoers. They soon took up enough of the gang prepared to turn king's evidence to obtain magistrates' warrants for the arrest of the leaders.

Late one night in October 1826 a party of some forty coast blockade men, led by Lieutenant Samuel Hellard, RN, and accompanied by Ruthven and an assistant, stole into the village of Aldington. The arrest operation had been carefully planned. As Lieutenant Hellard wrote afterwards in his report (quoted by E. Russell Oakley, see bibliography):

> Every house in which I expected to arrest a prisoner was surrounded by sentinels nearly at the same moment. I then instantly advanced to the house of George Ransley, the leader of this ruffian band, and was fortunate enough to get so close to his house before his dogs were disturbed that he had not time to leave his bed. The Dogs were cut down, and his door forced. Then I rushed in and had the satisfaction to seize the man in his bedroom. Having handcuffed him to one of the stoutest men in the Party, I proceeded to the other houses, and was equally successful in arresting seven others of the gang, whose names I subjoin.

The eight smugglers, together with others who were arrested subsequently, were convicted at Maidstone Assizes and sentenced to transportation for life. The Aldington Gang was no more.

From the early 1800s, it had been the practice to detach a boat's crew from each of the cutters and put them ashore at the worst smuggling spots with orders to carry out patrols offshore, particularly during the hours of darkness. These 'preventive boats' soon became an established and important arm of the Revenue service. The preventive 'Waterguard', as it came to be called, soon began to usurp the position formerly occupied by the Revenue cutters as the principal defence against the smugglers. (The term 'Waterguard' was until 1972 still used for uniformed Customs officers, somewhat incongruously in the case of staff employed at airports.)

In 1822, by an Order in Council, the entire coastline of England was divided for administrative purposes into three huge districts. District 1 extended from Land's End to Carlisle; district 2 from Land's End to the North Foreland; and district 3 from the North Foreland to Berwick. Each district was made the responsibility of an Inspecting Commander, who was responsible to the Board of Customs. They were exhorted thus:

> You are to observe that one material object of the duty imposed upon the Inspecting Commanders is to see that the cruisers are constantly and regularly on their stations, unless prevented by some necessary and unavoidable cause, and with their proper complement of their men and boats, and if they are off their station or in port personally to examine into the occasion of their being so, and that they are absent from their station no longer than is essentially requisite.

The districts were sub-divided into stations, each under the command of a chief officer. The authorised complement for each station consisted of a chief boatman, two commissioned boatmen and four boatmen. The boats themselves were generally three-masted, six-oared luggers; equipped with creeping-irons and a small-arms chest.

The chief boatmen, in their turn, were reminded: 'As night is the time when the smugglers generally run their cargoes, it is expected that the boat, or the crew, or the greater part of them will be out, either afloat or on land, as often as circumstances will permit, which must be, at least, five nights a week.'

The senior man in command of a boat was called the 'sitter', presumably because he sat in the sternsheets and did not pull an oar. Some chief officers, to ensure that their crews were diligent in patrolling, required sitters to take soundings along the tracks allotted to them, and to return a list of these when they went off watch. In inclement weather when rowing guard was not practicable, the crews were to keep watch ashore.

Now there existed three tiers of preventive forces along the coast. First the Revenue cutters, including men-of-war, patrolling the Channel and the North Sea, challenging vessels encountered at sea, boarding and rummaging suspect craft. Then came the preventive boats, rowing close inshore, searching creeks and inlets and keeping a general look-out for runs along the coastline. Finally, there were the 'Riding Officers' on land; these were Customs officers mounted and armed, whose function was to co-operate with their colleagues afloat by gathering intelligence, acting as a link between boat-stations, and intercepting successful runs which, having overcome the first two hurdles, were making their way inland to the distribution points.

One factor which had added nothing to the increased efficiency of

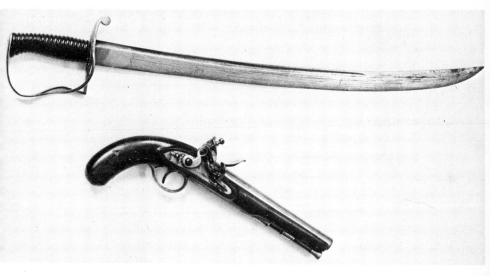

A Riding Officer's arms; standard issue sword and pistol.

the Revenue service up to 1822 was the plethora of administrative authorities with a finger in the Customs pie. At sea the preventive Waterguard, a naval force, was under Admiralty control; but the cutters, some naval and some civilian, were all under the Board of Customs. Ashore was the coast blockade, naval, but answerable to the

Treasury, and the Riding Officers (Landguard) sometimes assisted by the military. In addition to all these were the old port-based, purely Customs grades of surveyor, tide-waiter, and so on.

The Coastguard 1822-56

The core of the new service, named the Coastguard, was the old preventive Waterguard, now extended round the entire coastline but concentrated in the most vulnerable areas of the south, south-east and south-west. The head of the Coastguard was the Comptroller-General, a Captain of the Royal Navy on secondment. His headquarters office was situated in the London Custom House, and he was directly responsible to the Board of Customs.

Administration of the cutters remained with the Board, but the crews were selected by the Admiralty. Standards of entry into the service as commander or mate were raised; an applicant for a commander's billet was required to undergo a stringent examination of his competency as seaman and pilot. The Board directed that:

> . . . all persons who shall hereafter be nominated to the situation of Commander or Mate in the service of this Revenue do attend the Surveyor of Sloops, &c. in London for the purpose of being examined on the several points submitted in the report of the said Surveyor, as essential for the qualification of officers of that description, namely, whether he understands navigation, is competent to lay off and ascertain courses and distances on the charts, can work a day's work and find the time of high and low water in any port of Great Britain, and understand the use of a quadrant.

This applied only to civilian officers; the professional competence of their naval counterparts was taken for granted. A candidate otherwise qualified who lacked familiarity with the stretch of coastline that was to be his 'beat' was allowed to ship as a supernumerary in another cutter on the station until he had learned the necessary pilotage.

The cutters' men were for the most part competent and experienced seamen, recruited locally from seafaring communities. A naval rating wishing to transfer was required to have completed six years' service with the fleet, and to be of exemplary character. The crews were therefore a mixture of naval and civilian personnel. Those appointed by the Board of Customs were civilians, and they retained that status. They were not interchangeable with seamen manning the fleet, as were their naval colleagues. However, the 1822 Consolidation Act was the first of a successsion of measures which were to strengthen and extend Admiralty control of the Revenue cutters, and the civilian element was soon to disappear. From this date the cutters were merely a branch of the Coastguard; they were to remain so until their decline in the middle years of the century, when smuggling was much reduced.

The establishment of the Coastguard introduced an efficient central administration, and ended the 'amateur' era in the cutter service which had reached its apogee with the contract system. Henceforth, equipment and manning was standardised and the Inspecting Commanders ashore ensured that the cutters were deployed to the best advantage. The new authority inherited a total of sixty-nine ex-contract cutters; these were placed for administrative purposes in three classes, depending upon tonnage. The largest was the *Greyhound* stationed at Beachy Head. She was of 200 tons burden, mounted 16 guns and carried a crew of 43. The smallest was *Nimble*, 42 tons, with 15 crew and stationed at North Foreland.

A flood of regulations and instructions poured forth from the Comptroller-General's office (Instructions to Coastguard, 1832):

> They are to cruise diligently on the station alloted to them, not remaining in any harbour, bay, or creek, longer than compelled by any casualty or stress of weather, or than may be actually requisite for the due execution of their orders, and for the benefit of the public service. It is a most important part of their duty to keep the sea in bad weather and during the night, such being generally preferred by the smugglers for their operations.
> They are, during the day, to keep a good offing, and as much as possible

out of observation from the land, closing in towards the evening, and keeping as near the shore as may be practicable by night.

and:

It being of great importance to the Service that Cruizers should be thoroughly efficient at the commencement of the autumn, and all necessary repairs and refitments completed, the District Commanders are to make such arrangements as will ensure the attainment of this object, observing that no general refit will be allowed between the 1st. October and the 1st. April, except in consequence of some considerable and unforseen casualty.

Revenue cutter *Viper* passing the Gunfleet Beacon.

This last, of course, was to ensure that the cutters were up to strength during the winter smuggling season. The major refits were carried out at Deptford, but District Commanders were authorised to incur expenses for minor repairs, in order that they could be carried out locally.

The Coastguardsmen manning the shore stations received their due share of regulation, needless to say. No boatman was to be employed at a station which was less than twenty miles from his home, so that he should not be seduced from the path of duty by friends and neighbours; he was to reside as near as possible to his place of duty but he was not to lodge with smugglers (not easy, this!). He was not permitted to own his own boat. Any boatman marrying into the family of a known smuggler was to be reported to the Board. All these strictures reflect the Board's determination that the Coastguard should not be 'got at' by the smugglers; no doubt the dubious reputation earned by the coast blockade was in their minds. The following excerpt illustrates a recurring theme in instructions to the Coastguard: 'Officers of Stations are to be particularly cautious not to give rest to too many of the Men, under the impression that violence of the weather and state of the coast or beach render a landing impracticable; always bearing in mind, that the smugglers wholly disregard the loss of their boats, provided they can run their goods.' No detail was overlooked; one instruction was that 'every Officer and Man in the Coastguard should be able to make a shrill loud whistle'. In those days when dental care was not what it is now, this requirement must have disqualified many otherwise suitable men who, for one reason or another, were lacking their front teeth.

The most usual method employed by the Coastguardmen to alert each other to the presence of smugglers, was to fire warning shots from pistols or muskets. It was found necessary to instruct them that, when coming suddenly upon a party of smugglers, they were not to fire off *all* their small arms in sounding the alarm, as they would thereby leave themselves defenceless.

The Royal Navy was now responsible for Revenue stores and equipment. The initiated will recognise the voice of the eternal naval stores officer in the following:

General Memorandum. Coast Guard Office, 29 August 1829. Many of the Spying Glasses supplied to Cruizers and Stations have been returned to this Office in a state highly discreditable to the Officers, some of them having the glasses inverted, others having the glasses misplaced, and many with the worms of the screws broken, which appears to have been done by violence . . .

In spite of the increased efficiency of the Revenue force, there was no immediate reduction in the volume of smuggling; indeed, during the early 1820s it rose to new heights. But the following House of Commons return of goods seized by all branches of the preventive service from 1822 to 1824 inclusive bears witness to their effectiveness:

129 vessels; 746 boats; 312 head of livestock; 135,000 gallons of brandy; 227,000 gallons of gin; 10,500 gallons of whisky; 253 gallons of rum, and 596 gallons of wine. 3,000lbs snuff; 19,000 lbs. of tea; 42,000 yds. of silk; 21,000 Indian handkerchiefs; 36,000 packs of playing cards; 75 spirit stills and 23 Leghorn hats.

(The whisky was presumably seized by Excise officers from illicit stills.)

The Coastguard, as its name implies, was largely a land-based force patrolling cliff-tops and beaches and maintaining a 'rowing guard' close inshore. A comparatively small proportion of its establishment was employed in manning the Revenue cutters. The Coastguardman must have become a familiar figure in the 1830s, patrolling his beat along lonely cliff paths, armed with musket, spy glass and one-legged 'donkey stool' (a plebian variety of shooting-stick) on which he would rest from time to time to scan the horizon. The donkey stool was considered a valuable aid to Revenue alertness; if its user should chance to nod off, he was deposited smartly upon the ground.

Unlike the coast blockade, the Coastguard was not often called upon to tackle the smugglers in force. By 1830 armed gangs were rarely encountered; a decade later, smuggling had begun its great decline

A detachment of dragoons intercepting smugglers in the act of running a cargo.

and the Coastguard, under-employed in its Revenue function, began to evolve into a mere naval auxiliary.

The main reason for the change is not far to seek: the United Kingdom was embarking upon an era of Free Trade; tariffs were greatly reduced or altogether removed on a vast range of goods, including spirits, the smuggler's stock in trade. The trend had begun even earlier. In 1815, at the end of the French wars, no fewer than 1,425 commodities were subject to duty; by 1822, there remained only a score or so.

The Industrial Revolution, and the improvement in communications with the building of railways, also had its effect in reducing the demand for manufactured goods hitherto not readily obtainable by licit means in remote coastal areas. The formation of the Coastguard and increased efficiency in the preventive services contributed to the decline of smuggling to some extent; though the smuggler would certainly have found the means to satisfy the demand had it existed still.

The Coastguard Service from 1856

How were the Revenue cutters affected by the decline in smuggling? The Coastguard had had effective control of the cutters from its establishment in 1822, and although the Board of Customs was nominally the administrative authority, through the Comptroller-General of the Coastguard, in practice it had little say in matters affecting the maritime preventive service, which became increasingly the prerogative of the Royal Navy. In 1856 the position was regularised by the passing of the Coastguard Service Act, which made the Coastguard a branch of the Navy, and relieved the Board of Customs of any responsibility for it. Under this Act the Coastguard's functions were defined as: firstly the defence of the realm; secondly, the efficient manning of the fleet; thirdly and lastly, protection of the revenue. Henceforth, the majority of Coastguardmen were to be naval reservists, fully trained as such and ready to man ships of the fleet at short notice; but outside times of national emergency they were to be employed in the prevention of smuggling. The cutter fleet was greatly reduced in number; most of the older ones were sold or laid up.

The Navy was taking over a pretty mixed force, and was not entirely happy about it. Civilian personnel were gradually pensioned off or discharged. They were, of course, an embarrassment; it was quite impractical to have some members of a cutter's crew subject to naval discipline and others not, now that the cutters were primarily warships.

Some senior naval officers were sceptical of the Coastguard's effectiveness as a force for repelling invasion in those days of steam-driven warships. Rear Admiral HRH The Duke of Edinburgh writes in 1880:

> It must be remembered that in 1831 Steam was in its infancy, that England had but 1 or 2 Steam Sloops, and a very few smaller vessels; whilst other Nations had no Steam Navy at all. Whereas it would probably be considered at the present day, the Men of the Coast Guard *whilst on shore*, could

scarcely even enter into any calculation for defence, or be any even slight resistance against any future attempt at Landing, with all the power, precision, and celerity, which is afforded by Steam in its present gigantic development.

Naval strategists then, and later, tended to over-estimate the likely effects of new techniques on the realities of war.

The new service was not popular with officers and men of the fleet. Promotion prospects were poor, and with the general decline in smuggling there were fewer opportunities to earn seizure rewards. The Coastguard tended to attract elderly officers, looking for a quiet billet in which to end their days in the service, and it became known contemptuously throughout the Navy as 'the refuge for the destitute'. A list of establishments dated March 1856 revealed that of 148 lieutenants employed in the Coastguard, 51 were aged between fifty and sixty, and no fewer than 56 were over sixty.

The same list reveals a total of 95 'civilian' officers on the Coastguard strength, drawn from the mercantile marine and the East India Company. Of these, 60 were cutter commanders and mates. There was often friction and ill-feeling between the naval and civilian element, a major cause of it being that the latter received less pay than their naval equivalents filling similar posts. The lieutenants also were jealous of their juniors in rank, the mates, who, though merely warrant officers, could be promoted after five years' cutter service to chief officers of stations and were then ranked equivalent to lieutenants.

The Coastguard Service Act of 1856 decreed that the aged and infirm among the personnel were to be pensioned off; those approaching retirement age could be retained until they had qualified for a pension. It placed all personnel under naval discipline and made them subject to naval punishment for misdemeanours. The men were to be drilled regularly on the 'great guns' with which fleet ships were armed.

Under the re-organisation, the entire coastline of the British Isles, including Ireland, was divided into eleven districts, each under the

107

command of a captain of the Royal Navy. In each district a man-of-war 'guardship' was stationed, to which the Revenue cutters were attached as tenders. The cutters were manned from the complement of the guardship, and the crews were to be kept at such a pitch of training that they could be readily transferred back to the fleet when necessary.

The system of manning the cutters with bluejackets gave rise to some criticism. The Duke of Edinburgh, on resigning command of the Coastguard and reserves in November 1882, wrote in his valedictory report: 'It is not to be expected that seamen trained on board iron-clads would make good cutter-sailors; besides, the men of the Fleet are accustomed to strict discipline; the cruizers having no police, there is not the same watch over the men, and the punishments are more numerous than in former years in these vessels.' He suggested that the cutters should recruit newly entered boys—preferably the sons of Coastguardmen. 'The present officers of cruizers', he wrote, '. . . are mostly from this source. They become first rate pilots, and although their vessels are at sea in all weathers, in most dangerous navigation, the English Channel, there is hardly a case on record of any disaster, not one for many years at any rate.'

The Coastguard, ashore and afloat, continued as an active fleet reserve. By the turn of the century, the revenue fleet was much reduced. In December 1909, there remained only six revenue cutters. These were: the *Squirrel* (North Sea and eastern half of the English Channel); *Argus*, *Julia* and *Fanny* (Cornwall, Devon and western half of the Channel); *Thrush* and *Colleen* (Irish waters). Even these few were not fully occupied in preventive work; they combined their Revenue duties with fishery protection. It is an indication of the extent to which smuggling had diminished by this date, that a single cutter was considered adequate to guard the whole of the east and south-east coasts. Admiral Sir Reginald Henderson, on relinquishing his command, reported that 'Revenue protection work consists principally in preventing illicit trafficking with Coopers. Two Dutch coopers were arrested by *Argus* in 1905 and condemned and one Dutch cooper was arrested by *Skipjack* in May 1907 and condemned.' Three coopers in as many years seems a small enough haul even for those law-abiding times; the Admiral was perhaps being somewhat over-complacent about the state of smuggling. There still remained a few high-duty goods, notably tobacco, and it is difficult to believe that little or none was being smuggled. Nevertheless, according to the Admiral, 'The Coast Guard have not had to deal with any attempts at smuggling on a large scale, and, except for about a dozen cases of minor smuggling of small quantities of tobacco or liquor, their preventive duties have been

Officers and crew of Revenue cutter *Vigilant*, 1906.

of a purely passive nature, but no doubt their presence acts as a deterrent.'

In July 1914, with war-clouds gathering, the fleet was mobilised and the Coastguard went to war. The cutters' men went to their war stations and the Royal Navy took over contraband control duties. The older men were retained to man the look-out stations ashore, and performed valuable service in spotting and reporting those two new weapons in the naval armoury, magnetic mines and submarines.

1923 was a significant year in that it saw the establishment of the Coast Preventive Service. This was a department of the Customs, and consisted of a body of men, mostly naval pensioners, whose duty it was to patrol the coastline on the look-out for runs, much as the old Coastguard had done. But there were far fewer of them, and each of the Coast Preventive men, as they were titled, had thirty or forty miles of coastline to patrol singlehanded. From this date, the Coastguard relinquished its Revenue protection function entirely (apart, of course, from routine co-operation with the CPM patrols) and became, as it is at the present day, primarily concerned with the safety of shipping around the coast.

Smuggling showed a flicker of life in the 1930s. The Import Duties Act of 1932 reimposed tariffs on some commodities, more to protect them from foreign competition than to raise revenue. But the Depression was in full swing (if that is the right word), money was short and there was little demand for luxuries. However, those in a position to know about these things had a different story to tell. A mercantile marine captain, speaking at a conference of master-mariners at Southampton in 1933, said:

> Between Dungeness and Hastings there is a large tract of shore, lonely and unguarded except for widely-spaced coast watchers. Similarly the waste of coast in the vicinity of Selsey Bill has inlets which afford easy access to the shore for small vessels—a fact which has been evidenced by prosecutions. In some instances the smugglers have tried to take in whole cargoes.

The sole Revenue cutter in service during the 1920s, before and after conversion. Yet another *Vigilant*, she was formerly HM trawler *Esther*.

Another aspect of illicit traffic in the 1930s strikes a topical note today. The Home Office was concerned at the number of illegal immigrants (estimated at 600 a year) being smuggled into the country. They were said to be carried in fishing boats from French ports, transferred in mid-Channel to British coasting vessels, and landed unobtrusively in minor ports where there was no immigration officer. These were not coloured Commonwealth immigrants, of course; they were European refugees from Nazi oppression, who for one reason or another had been unable to gain admittance to the United Kingdom through legitimate channels. Needless to say, this traffic was masterminded by faceless men operating in Continental ports, who, it was alleged, charged £60 per head for the passage.

During most of the inter-war period, a single Revenue cutter guarded the entire coastline of Britain from the depredations of smuggling. It was not until the post-war years brought with them a new golden age of contraband-running, that the Revenue cutters became once again a force to be reckoned with.

7

Encounters at Sea

I beg to report that the commander of the revenue cruiser, while cruising on this station yesterday, boarded and seized a Russian brigantine, the *Yohannes*, Capt. C. G. Shurman, with a crew of nine men, from Cadiz, bound for Elsinore.

Inspecting Commander's report: Folkestone, 30 April 1854

Cutters on Patrol

Smugglers and Revenue men did not exchange shots or blows as a matter of course on meeting. Nevertheless, armed clashes were not uncommon either on land or sea, and both sides prepared for that eventuality. The smugglers, in offering resistance to lawful arrest, branded themselves as violent criminals. They were audacious when the odds were in their favour; the hangman's noose awaited those who fought and lost. As the nineteenth century entered its second decade, public attitudes toward the smugglers were hardening. The smugglers themselves had helped to bring the change about, by their more outrageous forays against the forces of law and order; a nation locked in war against a revolutionary state began to look less kindly on its own delinquents—especially those who had earned a reputation, as smugglers undoubtedly had, for seditious dalliance with the enemy. (Would it be cynical to suggest that the removal of customs dues on many imported commodities had any bearing upon the change in public sympathies?) Juries began to convict the patently guilty, and the revenue men went about their duties with greater confidence.

A truly marathon sea chase is recorded in 1806, culminating in the seizure of the *Lottery* cutter by the *Hinde* revenue cruiser, stationed at Fowey. *Lottery*, owned and commanded by a Cornish smuggler of some notoriety—one Thomas Potter, native of Polperro—had some months previously been involved in a fracas in which a revenue officer was shot dead. For that reason, if for no other, the preventive forces in the southwest were keeping a sharp lookout for the *Lottery*. Their patience was rewarded one late autumn afternoon, when *Hinde*'s crew sighted her off the Devon coast, making for the shore. *Hinde* put out to head her off, and a long pursuit began.

Lottery was a fast vessel of her type and on this occasion very skilfully handled. She tacked away down Channel, zig-zagging close inshore and out again, with *Hinde* doggedly following in her wake. Night came on and the chase continued: *Hinde* staying close but never quite getting within gun range. When dawn broke the wind dropped, as it often does at first light, and both vessels lay becalmed some six cables distant from each other.

The revenue cutter sent her boats away in charge of the mate. *Lottery* got her sweeps out and attempted to pull away, but *Hinde*'s boats soon pulled alongside. As they did so the smuggler opened fire on them with small arms and (having in mind, no doubt, the earlier shooting incident) the mate felt it politic to retire. He returned to the cutter, and as the first breeze rippled the smooth sea both vessels got under way.

For several hours, in light winds, the chase continued, but as the day wore on *Hinde*, barely perceptibly, began to close the gap. *Lottery's* crew in desperation jettisoned much of their cargo, but to no avail. By mid-afternoon, the wind being steady, the revenue cutter had closed to within range of her swivel-guns. She fired a warning shot which splashed into the water close by the smuggler's bows. Her crew, seeing at last the game was up, launched a boat and abandoned ship. *Hinde's* commander sent a heavily-armed party after them in his two boats; this time the smugglers surrendered without offering resistance. They were later tried and convicted at Exeter Assizes. No one was charged with the murder of the customs officer, for lack of evidence.

On a dull overcast January morning in 1817, His Majesty's schooner *Pioneer* was engaged in a revenue patrol off Dungeness. At two o'clock in the morning her commander, Lieutenant John Rouse, sighted a lugger under full sail about six miles to the north-west, making for the English coast. Rouse sent away two of his boats, with orders to head off the suspect craft.

As the larger of the two approached her, the lugger hoisted out her tub boat, which pulled away strongly to seaward. When the officer in charge of *Pioneer's* boat boarded the lugger he found only two men remaining on board; these he transferred to *Pioneer* when she subsequently arrived at the scene. Lieutenant Rouse questioned the two; one man claimed to be Dutch and the other French. The latter spoke not a word of his 'native' tongue but was fluent in English, which was hardly surprising as his name was William Stephenson. He eventually admitted that of the crew of eight (the other six had escaped in the tub boat) five were English, himself included, and three Dutch.

The lugger was rummaged, and was found to be carrying a full cargo of geneva, tobacco and tea, made up into small parcels for landing. Lieutenant Rouse, having carefully taken bearings to establish that he was inside the prescribed limits, formally seized the lugger and her cargo.

The ship's papers were false, as they showed her bound for Bilbao.

The lugger was really just a large open boat, having no decks and fitted with oars. It was unlikely, to say the least, that such a craft would venture a crossing of the Bay of Biscay in mid-winter. Further search revealed a paper which incriminated the smugglers beyond question. It read as follows:

For B. Valden
From Tusca Tower to Blackwater Hill, allowing half a point for the tide.
F. W. Martenson Glyn.
From Tusca N.E. until Tar Hill bears N.W.
At Clocker Head, Bryan King
At the Mountain Fort, Henry Curran ...

with other equally cryptic notations.

The document was, in fact, a 'spot-note'. The 'spotsman' was an important member of a smuggling crew, his function being to select a landing place for the contraband, using his local knowledge of tides, currents, and the likelihood or otherwise of revenue interference. The places listed in the above paper were all on the south and south-west coast of Ireland, to which the goods were consigned. Sailing directions were included.

The lugger was taken into Dover, where her cargo was impounded in the king's warehouse. The Dutchman was set free, but Stephenson was gaoled in Dover Castle, from whence he later contrived to escape. The remainder of the crew made good their escape to France in the lugger's boat.

On 11 May 1818, HMS *Florida* was cruising in the Straits of Dover. Her commander ordered away a boat in charge of Mr Keith Stewart, master's mate, with instructions to intercept any suspicious craft approaching from the French coast. Stewart patrolled for some hours without incident until, at 1 am, when about six miles northwest of Cap Blanc Nez, he sighted a large galley under sail and oars, steering to the westward. She later proved to be the *St Thomas* of Deal.

He pulled alongside and hailed her. Her steersman answered the traditional hail, 'What boat, and where bound?' by enquiring the identity of Stewart's boat. He was obviously playing for time, as the mate was in full uniform and his boat wore the customs ensign. Stewart ordered him to lower his sails, to which command he responded by urging his oarsmen to pull harder. Stewart warned him that if he did not heave to, he would open fire.

'Fire and be damned', bellowed the steersman. 'We are as well armed as you are!'

Stewart held his fire, but ordered his crew to pull close alongside the St Thomas, telling her skipper as he did so that he intended to board. His bowman grappled the galley's gunwhale with his boathook, which was promptly knocked aside. Stewart clambered forward and, ordering his coxswain to follow him, leapt aboard the smuggler, to find himself looking down the muzzle of the steersman's pistol. Stewart fired first, and the man fell to the deck. The galley's crew abandoned their oars and crowded aft, menacingly. Meanwhile, Florida's boat had lost her precarious hold on the St Thomas and had drifted some distance away, leaving the two revenue officers in a perilous situation.

Stewart drew his sword and ordered the smugglers forward. Two men rushed at him and he slashed them both; the rest drew back. The Florida's crew soon pulled back alongside and, securing their boat, climbed aboard. In the ensuing search they found that the galley was laden with 207 kegs of tobacco, slung and weighted ready for sinking. Of the crew of thirteen, seven were English, including the three injured; the rest were Dutch.

The skipper lay where he had fallen, mortally wounded. He asked to speak to Stewart, and said, 'You've killed me, sir—I'm dying.' Stewart replied, 'Well, I'm sorry for it, but it was your own fault.' 'I know that', said the dying man, 'I freely forgive you for it. I hope you won't make things worse than they are.'

The St Thomas, together with her cargo and her dead captain, was taken into Great Yarmouth (Florida's station) and turned over to the

Collector of that port. She was found to be 54ft in length, which was exceptional for an undecked boat under oars. She also carried three lugsails and a jib, and must have been capable of a good turn of speed.

Cutters at War

A little known aspect of the Revenue service's employment was the part it played in various wars, big and small, armed expeditions and the like. Whether under Admiralty jurisdiction or not, the cutters were always armed vessels in government service. Frequently, during a state of hostilities when their preventive function was of a non-urgent nature, they were diverted to fill more war-like roles.

The Revenue department's outstanding battle honour was the ill-fated Walcheren expedition of 1809, when no fewer than fourteen Revenue cutters were included in the supporting fleet. They performed a vital function, being responsible for the small boat work of ferrying the troops and their supply train ashore; several of the crews distinguished themselves in individual acts of valour.

As far back as the early 1700s, cutter commanders had been granted letters of marque to act as privateers against the enemy of the day. They were thus authorised to board and seize any vessel under enemy colours encountered on the high seas and, more important from their point of view, entitled to prize money for doing so. Not surprisingly, letters of marque were much sought after. The risks were not great, as few merchantmen were formidably armed, even in wartime, and the rewards were high.

The Board was not over enthusiastic. They feared, rightly, that zeal for the Revenue might be subordinated to a thirst for prize money. They emphasised that they would not bear any part of the expense of repairing damage sustained in taking prizes-of-war where no Revenue consideration was involved; any such damage was to be made good by the commanders themselves. Also (and somewhat optimistically) they urged the commanders not to neglect their preventive duties, or to leave their stations 'under pretence of looking for captures, it being our resolution to recall the permission hereby granted, as soon as it shall be discovered in any instance to be prejudicial to our service'.

When a prize was taken, it was brought into harbour by its captors; the crew was interned and the vessel, together with its cargo, was sold to the highest bidder. The amount realised, plus a sum of 'head money' for each enemy alien in the crew, formed the basis of the prize money. A small percentage was deducted to cover expenses, and the balance was paid over to the commander and crew. The share-out was in the following proportions, laid down by a Royal Warrant dated 11 June 1795:

```
The Commander  .............14/32nds
The Mate  .....................7/32nds
Deputed Mariner ...............3/32nds, exclusive of his share as Mariner
Other Mariners ................8/32nds
```

Small wonder, with such pickings, that the cutters were anxious to earn their share. The enemy merchantmen, also, tended to be much less formidable than a determined smuggler, armed to the teeth and looking for trouble.

Not that privateering was entirely without risk. Captain Francis Sarmon of the *Swan* cutter, whom we encountred earlier (see p 41), took out a letter of marque in 1793. (This *Swan* was the third of that name, a converted smuggling vessel of 120 tons.) For two years he successfully and profitably combined smuggler-catching with the culling of prizes. But on 14 October 1795 his luck ran out.

Since early that year, the *Swan* had been detached on naval duties, together with other Revenue cutters, first in attendance on Admiral Duncan's fleet blockading the Texel and subsequently under Commodore Sir John Warren at the landing in Quiberon Bay (a naval expedition undertaken in support of French royalist insurgents against the Revolution).

It was during the latter foray that Sarmon was ordered to England with despatches. He was still just off the French coast when his lookout sighted three large ships a few miles ahead. Sarmon took them to be British frigates which he knew to be in the area, but as he closed to within gun-shot they hoisted French colours and called on him to surrender. In the circumstances he had little choice, and, having first destroyed the despatches, he struck his colours. The *Swan* was escorted into harbour, and Sarmon and his crew were imprisoned. They were repatriated in January 1796. Meanwhile, the *Swan* was put into service as a privateer under the French colours and re-named *La Bayonnaise*. She served as such until February 1799, when she was re-taken by the British.

For a ship like *Swan III* to have such a chequered career was by no means unique in those eventful days. Her crew, no doubt, accepted their setback with a good grace; it was the fortune of war. Sarmon, skilled seaman and doughty fighter as he was, acted at least as much from motives of profit as of patriotism. When the odds were obviously well against him, he surrendered—to go down with colours flying was no part of a privateer's code.

On this occasion he lived to fight another day; but not for long. On his return to England from captivity in 1796, he took command of a new *Swan* and resumed his freebooting activities. In December of that year, his ship was captured by a Frenchman after a fierce engagement in which Sarmon was killed. He died fighting, 'Killed by a musquett shot which struck him in the fore-part of the head', as one of his crew was later to testify.

Sarmon's record of activity against the enemy was not unequalled among cutter commanders, although he was probably more daring and energetic than most. Several of his crew cheerfully served with him through good times and bad, including the period of incarceration in a French gaol, and were with him to the end. He was evidently a man whose qualities inspired devotion and was held in high esteem by his superiors.

Revenue cutter *Swan* (on left) engaged by French privateer *L'Unité*, December 1796; the action in which Captain Francis Sarmon was killed.

Other cutters active against enemy shipping at this time included the *Greyhound* stationed at Weymouth, the *Badger* of Harwich, and the *Tartar* of Dover, all of which took a number of prizes. The last-named, whose commander rejoiced in the name of Benjamin Jelly Worthington, spent the first few months of the war acting as tender to a man-of-war, and was well placed for a little prize-taking on her own account.

The merchant seaman of those days had enough to contend with, in all conscience, in the way of hardship and danger. War in Europe was a further and ever-present hazard. It often fell out that while he was engaged in some long voyage his homeland would be involved in war and he would find himself on his homeward voyage the legitimate prey of his country's enemy. If that enemy happened to be Great Britain, so much the worse for him, as her ships were everywhere and he must approach her shores as he drew near home.

The end of the French wars in 1815 brought a long period of peace to Europe, and a consequent dearth of prizes. The cutters returned to their anti-smuggling duties; with reluctance, no doubt. Seizure rewards were harder earned, and less frequently as a rule, than prize money. However, smuggling showed no sign of abatement, quite the reverse, and there was plenty of work for cutter crews with an appetite for it.

The next opportunity for easy pickings for the cutters was not to arise until 1854, when Great Britain went to war with Imperial Russia. This conflict produced no big fleet activity in northern waters although Russia possessed a considerable navy. But she had ambitions in the Mediterranean, and it was to deny her ships the use of the Sebastopol base that the British army landed in the Crimea. (Cutter crews served in this expedition; 3,000 of them were mobilised to man fleet tenders.) Russia also had a large merchant fleet, some of which had the misfortune to be caught in British harbours at the outbreak of hostilities; they were seized where they lay. Thirty-two Russian ships were seized in British harbours at the outbreak of war, most of them in Hull and Grimsby. Seizures were effected by the local port-based customs officers.

Towards the end of March 1854 Her Majesty's Consul at Oporto sent a despatch to the Admiralty, listing eleven merchantmen in that port belonging to Russia or her allies, all of them bound for ports in northern Europe. Their crews were presumably unaware of the latest development in European politics, for' on completion of cargo they duly sailed out and turned north, heading for the chops of the Channel. Meanwhile, the cutters along the Channel coast had been alerted. It was not long before reports of captures began to come in:

> *Argus* Revenue cutter, Spithead
> 21 April, 1854
>
> Sir,
> I have the honour to inform you that having, during the last night, guarded the eastern entrance of the Wight with this Steamer, and a boat at a suspected spot inside; and nothing suspicious seen, I steamed out after daylight to the offing in search of smuggling craft, and to examine vessels likely to have on board stores of war. At noon, after examining several vessels, I boarded the Russian barque *Froija* from Lisbon, bound for the Baltic laden with salt; and in pursuance of your confidential letter of the 15th instant, I have detained and towed her to this port; waiting your further instructions.
>
> J. S. W. Grandy, Commander.

Note that the Commander stresses that he was engaged in his preventive duties when he had the good fortune to fall in with his prize.

The *Argus* was one of the first steam-powered craft to go into Revenue service. She was launched in March 1852, and was originally named *Ferret*. She cost £10,210, was schooner-rigged and carried only two light guns, which indicates to what extent armed resistance by the smugglers was a thing of the past. *Argus* was to take two more prizes in the ensuing days.

One by one, the hapless Russians were gathered in as they battered their way up-Channel. None of the eleven broke through into the North Sea and none attempted to avoid the trap by staying in the Atlantic and passing north of the British Isles—no light undertaking, but surely preferable to capture. It is likely that they were simply unaware that war had been declared. Three were eventually restored to their owners on legal technicalities, but the remainder were condemned as prizes-of-war. The ships and their cargoes realised a total of over £16,000. Prize money was not paid out automatically; certain formalities had to be gone through. It was necessary for commanders to petition the Board of Customs, through the Comptroller-General, for their claims to be considered. Here we have the commander of *Argus* stating his case:

> The Memorial of Commander John S.W. Grandy R.N., Commander of Her Majesty's Revenue Cruiser *Argus* on behalf of himself, Officers & Crew. Humbly Showeth.
>
> That, in pursuance of your orders on 15th. April last, the steamer under my command proceeded to cruise in the English Channel, to intercept and detain Russian merchant ships, and succeeded in capturing three, viz. the barque *Froija* and brigs *Livonia* and *Zelus*, which vessels, with their cargoes, have been condemned as lawful prizes to their captors, and are now under sale.
>
> Your memorialist therefore respectfully begs you will be pleased to represent to the Honourable Board of Customs, that those prizes were captured through the conduct and vigilance on the part of this cruiser, as expressed in your letter to me, dated 25 April last [in which Grandy had been commended] and further begs you will move their Honours to intercede, on the behalf of the captors, with the Lords Commissioners of the Admiralty, that their Lordships may award the disposable proceeds of the prizes to the captors accordingly; and,
>
> Your memorialists &c.

Grandy had done extremely well to intercept no fewer than three of the enemy ships; no doubt the greater mobility which his engine gave him played its part. He was to be well rewarded; his three prizes realised a total of £6,327 6s 6d.

Grandy's share of this sum might seem a more than adequate payment for doing what was, after all, no more than his plain duty. But that was the system; like seizure rewards, prize money was the inducement which made a man's duty clear to him, and encouraged his diligence in performing it. It worked well, on the whole.

Steam Revenue cutter *Argus*, the Crimea War prize-taker. Note the Customs
ensign—at that date with a gold crown badge in the fly.

A strong argument against prize money, however, was the fact that
it gave rise to jealousy and a sense of grievance on the part of those not
included in the distribution of largesse. Such bounties had been paid
in the first instance to the crews of men-of-war after successful armed
actions which resulted in the capture of enemy vessels, and a measure
of personal risk was implicit. The rounding-up of unarmed merchantmen as they made their unsuspecting way homewards was a different
matter; it was simply a case of being in the right place at the right time.
We can sympathise with a cutter commander's superior officer who
felt that he had earned a slice of his subordinate's cake. Captain
Skipwith, Inspecting Commander at Folkestone, petitioned the Board
of Customs in September 1854, claiming that most of the prizes were
taken as a result of his, Captain Skipwith's, diligence. He had gone to

great lengths, he said, to gather intelligence of the Russian vessels' movements, and he implied that without his efforts the captures would not have been made. 'I had indeed a hope', he says, 'that in respect of my activity and foresight, I might be deemed to have acted in a manner deserving of special reward for any capture made by my officers, entirely through my instrumentality and intervention; and I therefore trust that in this case you will be pleased to make such recommendations in my favour as you may deem just and proper.'

The *Johannes* and her cargo were eventually sold for £857; the records do not reveal if Captain Skipwith got a share. One hopes that he did, after all his 'activity and foresight'.

However, the easy pickings were soon exhausted; within a few weeks of the outbreak of war, the Channel was swept clean of Russian shipping.

At the close of the Crimean War the Coastguard, which included the Revenue cutters, became an integral part of the Royal Navy (see p 106). The Navy assumed responsibility for the preventive service at sea—not a very arduous one, as we have seen, with the decline in smuggling.

It was to be nearly sixty years before the outbreak of the next European war in which Great Britain was involved, and the Revenue cutters, as such, were to have no part in that conflict.

8

Modern Smugglers

An ex-R.N.V.R. type, one of them, oddly enough. Bought the stuff in
Cherbourg on the pretext that it was for the *Vanguard:* before her South
Africa trip. Flew the White Ensign and loaded over there under the eyes of
the douane . . .

from the novel A Piece of Cake *by Charles Anthony*

In the period immediately after World War II, many factors combined
to escalate smuggling to its highest pitch for a hundred years. Post-war
tariffs were high, and no reader much over the age of forty will need
to be reminded of the 'austerity' era when everything but basic
necessities were in short supply. The stringencies accepted by a nation
engaged in total warfare were continued, for various reasons, to the
close of the dreary 1940s and beyond.

At this time thousands of young men were being demobilised from
the armed forces; many of them had 'lived dangerously' during their
war service and had no inclination to settle down again into humdrum
occupations. Some of these had held wartime commissions in the Royal
Naval Volunteer Reserve and had achieved command of a small ship,
minesweeper, motor gun-boat or landing craft. They had become

proficient in navigation and seamanship and had gained a useful knowledge of pilotage waters around the British Isles and the Continent. Restless, stricken with sea-fever, hard-earned gratuities burning a hole in their pockets, they were not slow to see the opportunities for a skilled seaman having a fast boat and a little capital at his disposal. The boats were easy enough to come by; the Admiralty were selling off hundreds of surplus small craft at very favourable prices—among them fast, capacious motor launches.

On the other side of the picture, the Customs Waterguard had given in full measure to the war effort, and most of the younger men had gone into the forces while their elders were employed in such vital wartime functions as contraband control and the victualling of convoys. (A few were seconded to a 'cloak and dagger' unit, employing their particular skills in checking the equipment of British agents bound for enemy territory.) In the immediate post-war years, therefore, the Waterguard was in the throes of reconstruction; re-training demobilised staff, recruiting to replace those who had not returned, and stretching its resources to cover the ports meantime. Thus all the conditions which obtained during the golden age of smuggling were present at this time: high tariffs, a brisk demand for luxury goods and an overstretched preventive force.

From 1946 to 1948 there was only one revenue cutter in commission. Yet another *Vigilant*, she was formerly the Royal Navy ('Isles' class) ocean minesweeper *Benbechula* (see illustration on p 129). The Board of Customs purchased her in 1946 for a mere £10,000. She was a giveaway bargain because she was unsuitable for conversion and the Navy could not find a commercial buyer. A condition of sale, in those early days of the 'cold war', was that she should be handed back to the Navy immediately in the event of a national emergency.

The single revenue cutter operating during the 1920s and 1930s had been manned by mercantile marine officers and crew, carrying only one or two Customs officers, an uneconomic arrangement from the Board's point of view. The new *Vigilant* was manned entirely by Customs personnel and commanded by a Waterguard officer. Her commander had spent the war years in the merchant navy, during which time he had obtained a foreign-going master's certificate. His crew were not officers of Customs in the full legal sense; they were members of the Customs Launch Service, seamen and engineers who man the Waterguard patrol craft in the port areas and estuaries. *Vigilant* would usually embark two preventive officers when engaged upon revenue patrols.

Her crew quarters were modified to provide rather less spartan conditions than her naval crew would have enjoyed, and a stateroom

'Isles' class armed trawler *Benbechula* before conversion.

was built on aft to accommodate the Board and other dignitaries on their occasional official cruises. She was, of course, an ocean-going vessel in every respect and had no difficulty in keeping the sea in all but the worst of weather. During her fifteen years in commission, until she was finally laid up in 1961, *Vigilant* steamed many thousands of miles in the revenue service; showing the flag and 'keeping the smugglers' heads down'. Having transformed an ex-naval hulk into an efficient revenue cutter worthy to bear the name of her predecessors, the commander handed over his ship to a mercantile marine officer and retired ashore. Whether he knew it or not, he had established an important precedent for the post-war years in putting his expertise at the Board's disposal.

By 1948 it was obvious that the running of contraband goods by sea was reaching a serious level, and the Board of Customs and Excise realised that the time had come to re-establish off-shore revenue patrols. Accordingly, they again approached the Admiralty, those august if somewhat undiscriminating ship brokers, with a view to purchasing suitable craft for their purpose.

They were offered two HDMLs (Harbour Defence Motor Launches) neat, handy little ships with a respectable turn of speed, plywood hulls, twin diesel engines giving a comfortable top speed of about 10 knots, and adequate accommodation for a crew of six. They were just what the Board had in mind, and after a minimal amount of conversion they were commissioned into the customs service and became His Majesty's Revenue cruisers *Valiant* and *Vincent* (the Board having decided that their craft should, in the tidy naval fashion, bear names beginning with the same initial letter).

Volunteers from within the Waterguard service were sought to man them, and there was no lack of qualified applicants. Indeed the ranks of the post-war Waterguard abounded with experienced seamen, navigators, radio operators and the like, who had gained their expertise in the various armed forces. Some ex-RNVR types, as we have seen, took to smuggling as a peacetime occupation; but many others, fortunately for the revenue, preferred to work within the law.

One such had had a brilliant wartime career in Combined Operations, and achieved the very rare distinction of two bars to his Distinguished Service Cross. Barely two years after demobilisation he found himself once more in command of a king's ship. His crew were Waterguard colleagues, preventive officers as he was, but delighted to be back in harness and serving under a distinguished officer.

Typical Free-Traders of the Period

Dawn Approach was a war-surplus Royal Navy harbour patrol launch, purchased from the Navy in August 1946. Her new owner had spent the war in Admiralty employment, attached to the Small Vessels Pool, and delivering small craft to various bases around the coast as they were required. After the war, he established himself in the same line of business, ferrying boats on behalf of private owners. He carried on a legitimate business for two years or so, but he was losing money and began to cast about for a means of recouping his losses.

The opportunities for running illicit cargoes had not escaped his notice, and he decided to chance his arm. He began with every advantage. He was well known to the Customs officers in those ports where small craft frequently called; known to them, that is, as an honest citizen making a living in the way he knew best. His comings and goings were necessarily haphazard; he had no particular base-port so his absence for days at a time would not attract notice.

His first venture in the trade took place in January 1949, when he picked up in Nieuport a cargo of imitation pearls and brought them into Ipswich, concealed in the ballast-tanks. He had no trouble in landing the contraband, and a month later ran a similar cargo at Great Yarmouth. Swiss watches, good, bad or indifferent, were a commodity assured of a ready market in Britain, with no questions asked; our man hastened to meet the demand. He was a painstaking smuggler, never content with his hiding-places which he realised would quickly be uncovered should the Customs begin to pay close attention to him. However, he discovered from the shipbuilder's detailed drawings, which he had acquired at the time of purchase, that the main transverse bulkhead between the saloon and the engine-room was hollow, possibly to allow for soundproofing, and gave access to a considerable space, ready-made for stowing illicit cargo.

During the year 1950 he made no fewer than sixteen undetected runs from Antwerp or Dunkirk, each time with a cargo of several thousand watches in the bulkhead, all to south or east coast ports. On the last of these trips he was disconcerted to be paid a visit by a Waterguard rummage crew, who carried out a thorough search. Nothing was found, but the preventive officers left behind them a very worried smuggler.

He tried unsuccessfully to convince himself that it had been a purely routine search, such as he might expect to be subject to from time to time, and decided to lay a false trail. For the next few months he would declare his destination to be the Republic of Ireland, but would stop en route on the south-east coast of England to deliver his contraband to an accomplice for transport to London, reporting himself at Dublin as arrived direct from the Continent.

But by now the Customs were on to him. Whenever *Dawn Approach* showed up in a United Kingdom port she was given special attention. They knew that her owner was smuggling in a big way; he knew that they knew, but was confident that they would not find his hiding-place in the hollow bulkhead. His confidence was not misplaced; the Customs searchers never did find it, but eventually, on 21 February 1951, it was revealed.

Customs Special Investigation Branch officers had for some months been taking a close interest in the movements of *Dawn Approach*. In

February 1951 a report was received from Cherbourg that a cargo of watches had been loaded near there. They were waiting at his destination, saw the contraband loaded into a car and followed to London, where they intercepted it and took 13,000 Swiss watches into custody. Also found in the car were papers which revealed the extent of the boat's smuggling activities, and, at last, the long-sought hiding-place. Her owner was finally brought to justice, fined heavily and imprisoned.

Another post-war recruit to the smugglers' ranks was the owner of *Taku*, a government surplus air-sea rescue craft. His war service had been rather more eventful than that of his colleague in *Dawn Approach*; he had been a submarine officer of some distinction. He was joined in

A Waterguard officer hails an arriving yacht on the river Hamble.

his enterprise by a few wartime friends of a like disposition, and they were soon active in the business of free-trading. Their principal stock-in-trade was French wines and liqueurs, of which, naturally, there was a severe shortage just after the war. Now, it is a happy chance that those who really appreciate the good things in life are often, in times of shortage, able to pay inflated prices in order to obtain them. (Ask any publican who in those years of drought had the problem of sharing out his meagre quota of Scotch whisky among his 'regulars'!)

Taku's owner and his friends were, to be fair to them, attempting to meet a demand; and curiously enough, did not set out to evade the lawful revenue payable on their cargoes. Indeed, they would have been perfectly happy to pay the duty, assured as they were of a handsome profit on even duty-paid wines and spirits at the inflated prices then current. Unfortunately, a far greater obstacle lay in the path of these benefactors of mankind than the mere requirement to 'render unto Caesar': this was government restriction on the movement of currency whereby legitimate importers were severely limited in the amount of sterling they were allowed to spend abroad, and import licensing was required for all but essential goods. It was this restriction, and not simple revenue evasion, which provided the main impetus to post-war smuggling.

Taku's method was to proceed to various French ports in turn to load her cargoes, masquerading as a ship of the Royal Navy. Her skipper and crew had the effrontery to represent themselves to the local bonded-stores merchants as serving naval officers engaged upon victualling missions on behalf of particular British warships (see quotation at head of this chapter). Between July 1946 and April 1947 *Taku* made many successful runs of liquor to various parts of the south coast, but then a tongue wagged and the Customs Investigation Branch were alerted. From that moment *Taku*'s free-booting days were numbered.

In the meantime, however, her skipper was prospering mightily.

He could hardly believe his luck—all his runs had been made without the slightest mishap or interference; no narrow squeaks for him such as *Dawn Approach* had experienced. He decided to expand the 'firm'. At the end of 1946, he chartered a government surplus landing-craft, LCM 217. He was well aware, as were his predecessors, that the most perilous part of any smuggling enterprise lay in landing the goods. There were many quiet stretches of beach on the south coast of England, ideal for his purpose, which he could not utilise because of *Taku*'s draught, and isolated beaches were less likely to be supervised by revenue patrol than harbours, however small.

LCM 217 was used on a number of occasions to land cargoes: cases of spirits were transferred from *Taku* in mid-Channel and run in, while *Taku*, innocent of contraband, proceeded into harbour. It was following such a rendezvous, in the early hours of the morning of 13 April 1947, that *Taku*'s run of luck ended. To speak of luck, though, does less than justice to the officers of the Customs and Excise Investigation Branch, who had been working assiduously to bring about the downfall of *Taku*'s skipper and associates, and whose agents in Cherbourg, Le Havre and elsewhere had been striving to piece together a full dossier of their activities. Armed with 'information obtained' the SIB men were ready and waiting as LCM 217 nosed on to the shingle at Arne Beach in Poole harbour on that April morning. The lorry conveying her cargo, over a hundred cases of spirits, was intercepted a little way inland and in due course all the smugglers were rounded up and brought to justice.

The Role of the Cutters

The misfortune which befell *Taku* and, a little later, *Dawn Approach*, combined with the tireless revenue activity of HMRC *Vincent* and *Valiant*, brought home to the smugglers that the game was becoming a little too risky. Moreover, import restrictions were being eased, albeit gradually, by the early 1950s, and customers were less ready to pay high prices with no questions asked.

The Revenue cutters, with few actual captures to their credit, were in fact filling to some effect the preventive role which the Board had envisaged for them. Who can say how many would-be smugglers were deterred from their purpose when on approaching harbour, at Calais perhaps, they received a cheerful wave from a uniformed figure on the deck of a craft flying (outside French territorial limits, of course) the British Customs ensign? And were hailed on their return in the politest Customs tones, and asked if they had been 'foreign' recently?

By 1960, the old *Vincent* and *Valiant* had steamed many thousands of miles between them in the Revenue service, and it was beginning to show. Mechanical failures were a regular occurrence, in spite of the ministrations of the preventive officers-cum-engineers, and the state of their wooden hulls was giving rise to concern—*Valiant*'s in particular had become alarmingly spongy. But already the Commissioners were proposing to establish a fleet of purpose-built Revenue cutters. *Vincent* and *Valiant* had proved their worth over the years and had conclusively shown once again that off-shore patrols were a necessary adjunct to the Revenue services. The streamlined Royal Navy no longer had any more-or-less suitable craft to sell off and it was necessary, for the first time for more than a century, to give thought to the design and construction of a Revenue cutter as such.

The first of the new vessels, *Venturous*, was launched from Messrs Philip's boatyard at Dartmouth in March 1962. Her somewhat unusual lines (see illustration opposite) excited a good deal of speculation and comment among onlookers at her various ports of call in the early days. Various fanciful interpretations were made of the initials HMRC emblazoned on her lifebuoys, ranging from 'rescue-craft' to 'rocket-carrier'. The knowledgeable no doubt recognised her blue ensign, defaced in the fly with the crown and portcullis badge.

A boarding party puts off from HMRC *Venturous*.

Venturous is 90ft long, displaces 120 tons, and is fitted with twin Paxman engines which give her a speed of 16 knots. She is equipped with the most sophisticated navigational aids, including high-definition radar which has proved its value on many occasions. The great improvement on the old cutters is in her extended range—*Venturous* can cruise 1,000 miles without refuelling, making possible longer patrols from base.

Her two consorts quickly followed: *Vigilant* (the tenth of that name) launched at Lowestoft in 1965, and a new *Valiant*, built at Thorne, Yorkshire, in 1968. *Venturous*, largest of the fleet, with a crew of eight, is based at Gravesend; *Vigilant* and *Valiant*, each with six, at Southampton and Plymouth respectively.

The commanders and crews, as before, are serving Waterguard officers who have volunteered for cutter-service. The post-war pool of qualified navigators, radio operators and engineers has long ago dried up, of course; most of those stalwarts have reached an age when the prospect of mid-winter revenue patrols has lost some of its appeal, though a few have stayed on to give younger colleagues the benefit of their wide experience.

But the volunteer spirit and the remarkable professional duality of the cutter crews are too valuable to lose. Accordingly, the Inspector-General of Waterguard seeks replacements for his crews among young Waterguard officers who, though perhaps lacking in technical qualifications and experience, possess keenness and readiness to learn. These officers are called upon as vacancies arise to serve in one or other of the cutters for a short period initially, in order that their seniors can assess their suitability, and also so that the new recruit can decide for himself if he measures up to the rigours of cutter service. If not, he is free to return to general port duties ashore, without prejudice to his future career.

The candidate who proves suitable is sent, at the Customs Department's expense, to the Marine Training School at RAF Mountbatten, Plymouth, where he undergoes a course in either seamanship and navigation or in diesel engineering, according to his talents and interest. The course gives him a sound training in fundamentals; he adds to his proficiency and gains experience aboard one of the cutters, under the guidance of the commander and senior engineer. Already trained as a Revenue officer, he is able to revert to that role instantly when required, putting aside the tools of his adopted trade to board and examine a suspect craft.

In this way, the future manning of the cutters seems assured. There is no lack of volunteers; indeed, there are enough trained crews to make possible any future expansion of the Revenue fleet. Meanwhile, the new cutters are proving their worth. Returns of goods seized from smuggling craft have once again taken an upward turn. Spirits and tobacco figure largely as ever, with (a sign of the times) drugs and illegal immigrants.

The latter-day cutter commander has the benefit of the best of modern equipment, but his task remains that of his forerunners: to patrol, challenge, board and search.

The case of *Fildon I* is worth recording because it provides an example of revenue success achieved by close co-operation between the various units involved, ashore and afloat.

Fildon I was a privately owned motor yacht belonging to an amateur yachtsman of impeccable respectability. In common with other yacht owners, he would occasionally hire out his boat on charter at such times as it would otherwise have been lying idle. In September 1967, one Van O——, a Belgian national and a twice-convicted smuggler, was released from his English prison. Unrepentant, he had it in mind to recoup his losses and approached *Fildon I*'s owner to negotiate a charter. The latter had no knowledge of his customer's background and terms were soon agreed. When, shortly afterwards, he was appraised of Van O——'s history, the outraged owner promptly informed the office of the Inspector-General of Waterguard that his craft had been hired by a smuggler.

Quite by chance, at this point Van O—— cabled the information that *Fildon I* had broken down in Dieppe. The owner crossed to Dieppe, accompanied by a mechanic. The mechanic's qualifications amounted to more than a knowledge of marine engines; he was, in fact, a Customs officer of the Special Investigation Branch. He duly repaired the engine and sailed in *Fildon I* to Nieuport, from whence he and his companion departed for England, leaving Van O—— on board.

Two Investigation Branch officers were already at Nieuport to see *Fildon I* arrive, and they settled back to watch and wait. They witnessed the contraband being loaded and assumed that Van O—— would shortly cast off from the quayside and set course for his destination. However, the smuggler seemed unready to do so; perhaps he felt that he had earned a few hour's sleep. The two watchers had been at their posts for most of the night and at 4am (there being no sign of activity aboard *Fildon I*) judged that it was safe to go off in search of refreshment. Returning an hour or so later, to their consternation they saw that the bird had flown. Their only means of contacting head-quarters was by telephone and the Bureau de Poste, of course, was closed.

They were still discussing what they should do when *Fildon I* re-appeared at the harbour entrance and tied up at her previous berth. It transpired later that she had been in collision with a fishing boat just outside the harbour, and Van O—— had put back to investigate suspected damage. However, nothing of consequence was amiss and *Fildon I* finally sailed at 7am.

The Investigation Branch men made their telephone call to London and various preparations were got under way to ensure that *Fildon I* should receive an appropriate reception committee. At the same time that the Investigation Branch officers were despatched to Nieuport, *Venturous*, then lying in Plymouth Sound, received orders to proceed to Dover, there to await news of *Fildon I*'s departure. Coastal patrols were alerted and mobile rummage crews were stationed at strategic points north and south of the Thames estuary.

As soon as word was received that *Fildon I* had put to sea, *Venturous* also sailed from Dover Camber. Her commander was in something of a quandary as he had no information as to his quarry's route and destination. Knowing Van O—— to be an inexperienced seaman and navigator, the commander made an astute (and entirely correct) guess that he would make his way close inshore down the French coast to Dunkirk and make the short crossing from there. *Venturous* steamed slowly towards Dunkirk, keeping a good look-out on all sides. In the late afternoon, some six miles off the French coast, *Fildon I* was sighted, heading cross-Channel. *Venturous* duly informed the other interested parties by radio-telephone and retired to a discreet distance. She fol-lowed *Fildon I* across to the South Goodwin lightship; up the east coast seaward of the Goodwins, and inshore towards the North

Foreland; passing from time to time a report of progress over the radio-telephone.

The North Foreland was rounded in darkness; *Venturous* barely a mile astern of *Fildon I* and with her lights extinguished. Her crew had begun to speculate that the landing was to be made somewhere in the Thames estuary, when quite abruptly *Fildon I* altered course towards Margate harbour. This caused something of a furore aboard *Venturous*, as at that point no radio contact could be made with the Investigation Branch unit ashore, who were in the process of shifting their position northwards from Deal. *Venturous* increased to full speed while her motor-boat was being turned out on its davit, and paused only to launch it.

At this most crucial of moments, radio-telephone contact was regained. The Investigation Branch unit quickly despatched a car to the harbour, which arrived there just as *Fildon I* was making fast to the jetty. The Investigation Branch men, together with the boarding-party from *Venturous* confronted a startled smuggler who at first denied possession of any contraband. A thorough rummage of the vessel revealed 20,000 or so Dutch cigars, concealed behind interior panelling and fittings in the saloon. Van O—— was duly charged with evasion of the duty and arraigned before a local magistrate. He was granted bail, but promptly made off, presumably to the continent, and at the time of writing is still at liberty.

Trends in Smuggling

No reader who takes a daily newspaper will be unaware of the alarming increase in drug smuggling which has manifested itself in recent years in most European countries, the United Kingdom not excepted. We may consider ourselves fortunate in Britain, if fortunate is the right word, that almost all illicit importations are of cannabis, a so-called 'soft drug'. The comparatively few seizures of heroin, morphine and cocaine intercepted at United Kingdom ports of entry are usually 'in transit' to the United States, where addicts are numbered in tens of thousands rather than in hundreds.

However, no country can afford to be complacent about drug-addiction; it is the most virulent of diseases. Addictive drugs, increasingly so in their modern concentrated forms, are difficult to detect unless in really large quantities. Many methods of evasion are employed: a seemingly ordinary passenger may disembark from a ship or aircraft with flat slabs of cannabis resin concealed about his person

Cannabis imported as freight and concealed in tins declared to contain cine film.

or in his baggage; a private motor car, one of perhaps two hundred such, may be driven ashore at a packet port with its chassis or door panels stuffed with drugs; a parcel from overseas may arrive at an inland address bearing a label declaring its contents to be 'books' or 'carved wood ornaments'. Customs officers today use sophisticated means to combat sophisticated smugglers. But those same customs officers, nothing if not realistic in such matters, would be the first to concede the old truth that where a demand exists and the profits are high, someone will be willing to meet the demand however great the risks. In some countries drug smugglers are summarily tried and shot; but the smuggling continues unabated.

The profits are vast. Ten kilograms of raw opium, costing at its source in Turkey, Thailand or Afghanistan about £150, increases dramatically in value as it is successively (and illicitly) refined into morphine base and then heroin. By the time it reaches its market it may realise £180,000. The profits on cannabis, though less spectacular, are still considerable. At source it costs £2 or £3 per pound weight; the price of that weight to the user would be not less than £250.

Cannabis, more often than not, is smuggled in a concentrated form known as cannabis resin, usually manufactured into flat cakes or slabs for easier concealment (see illustration on p 142). Early one January morning in 1970, the Pakistani motor vessel *Pussur* docked at Tilbury on arrival from Karachi. A preventive officer on routine rummage duties, walking the upper deck and sniffing the morning air, became aware of the distinctive odour of cannabis in the vicinity of the ship's funnel. Further investigation led to the discovery of over 400lb of cannabis resin, packed in sacks and concealed behind the insulated linings of the funnel. This, to date, is the biggest single *cache* of cannabis intercepted in the United Kingdom on shipboard (see illustration on p 144).

Another consignment which failed to reach the consumers arrived at Dover in November 1971: 370lb of cannabis concealed in the chassis of a 6-ton Volvo lorry (see illustration, p 145). This vehicle had been driven 6,000 miles overland from Kabul in Afghanistan. The Swedish driver declared the vehicle to be empty, which indeed it was, so far as its conventional freight capacity was concerned. But 6,000 miles is a long journey for a commercial vehicle to make without a payload of some sort, one might suppose. Anyway, the Customs officers thought so, but had literally to take the vehicle to pieces before finding the concealment. The Swede (who has gained fame of a sort by being the only lorry driver to take his night's rest at the Hilton Hotel, Brussels) was jailed, together with three English accomplices, for six years.

400 lb of cannabis resin slabs discovered aboard the Pakistani motor vessel *Pussur* at Tilbury, January 1970.

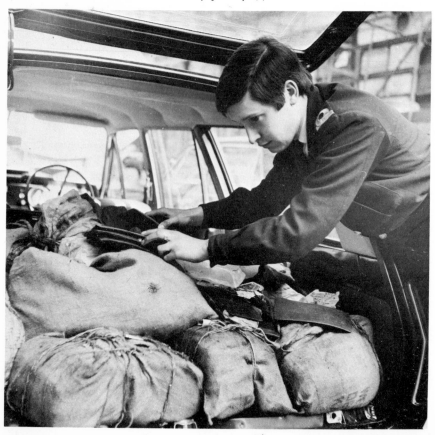

The container lorry from Kabul, seized and awaiting disposal at Custom House Quay, Pool of London.

I do not pretend, in the short space of this final chapter, to have covered all the many facets of smuggling today—smuggling by air, for instance, I have left to others—and indeed there is enough material to fill many books. The entry of Great Britain into the Common Market is bound, like other political and fiscal innovations in the past, to have its effect on the ancient craft of smuggling and on the commodities carried. But even after having 'gone into Europe' Britain remains an island in the geographical sense at least; whatever route the smugglers utilise they will not walk across her frontiers. The Channel Tunnel is still a dream, albeit one which may eventually be realised.

How convenient it would be for the British preventive men if all smugglers emerged from one pipe!

Glossary

BILL OF LADING: A shipmaster's detailed receipt to the consignor of a ship's cargo.

CABLE (CABLE'S LENGTH): A nautical unit of distance equal to one-tenth of a nautical mile, ie 200 yards.

CARVEL-BUILT: Used of a vessel the hull of which is constructed of planks laid edge to edge, providing a smooth outer surface.

CLINKER-BUILT: Used of a vessel the hull of which is constructed of overlapping planks, providing strength at the expense of speed, other factors being equal.

COLLECTOR: The principal Customs officer of a major port (often including a number of sub-ports). He is directly responsible to the Board of Customs.

COMPTROLLER: An official appointed by the Board of Customs to each Collectorship; subordinate to the Collector; his function being to ensure a proper return of duties etc collected.

CUTTER: Single-masted, fore-and-aft rigged craft with two or more headsails and fitted with a running bowsprit.

DANDY-RIGGED CRUISER: Cutter/sloop with jigger and small lug-sail.

DRAGOON: A mounted soldier, armed with sword and carbine.

EAST INDIAMAN: A merchant ship of the powerful East India Company. The company was chartered in 1660 and granted by the Crown exclusive trading rights in all places eastward of a line from the Cape of Good Hope to the Straits of Magellan; also allowed other privileges in respect of Customs duties. Privileges abolished in 1814.

GALLEY: Any large undecked boat propelled by oarsmen; with or without mast and sails.

GENEVA, GINEVA: Dutch brandy, introduced into England by William of Orange. Distilled from grain and flavoured with essence of juniper berries (hence 'gin').

HAT DUTY: A Customs duty of 5 per cent ad valorem imposed in 1660 on imported hats; repealed in 1861.

JIGGER: A small spar projecting over the stern to carry the foot of the mizzen sail outboard.

KING'S/QUEEN'S WAREHOUSE: A secure storage-place situated at a major port, in which contraband goods were held pending disposal.

LANDGUARD: The Revenue force known individually as Riding Officers; complementary to the Waterguard.

LUGGER: Two- or three-masted vessel carrying four-cornered sails bent to yards and laid fore and aft.

MASTER, RN: A warrant officer, descendant of the Tudor and Elizabethan 'Sailing Master', a pilot and navigator necessary in the days when the captain was probably a soldier with no pretensions to seamanship. Later, assistant to the captain in matters of navigation and ship-handling.

OWLER: A euphemism for the English wool smugglers, presumably because they were nocturnal in their habits.

PACKET-BOAT: A vessel employed in conveying passengers in or to and from any part of the United Kingdom.

RECEIVER OF WRECK: The collector or principal officer of a Customs port, appointed nowadays by the Board of Trade.

Glossary

SLOOP: Single-masted, fore-and-aft rigged vessel, usually with single headsail and fixed bowsprit.

SURVEYOR: The supervising officer of a Customs district.

SWEEP: A large heavy oar, manned by two or more men.

TANNED SAIL: A sail treated to render it rot-proof; a rich brown in colour.

TIDE-SURVEYOR: The preventive officer in charge of a boarding or rummage crew.

TIDE-WAITER: A shore-based Customs officer who boarded vessels on their arrival in port from foreign countries; now preventive officer.

ULLAGED CASE: ULLAGED CASK: A cask only partly full.

WATERGUARD SUPERINTENDENT: The senior officer in charge of a Waterguard division.

Bibliography

PUBLISHED SOURCES

Arnold-Foster, D. *At War with the Smugglers* (1936).

Baynham, Henry. *From the Lower Deck* (1969).

Carter, Captain Henry. *Autobiography of a Cornish Smuggler* (1900).

Cooper, William Durrant. 'Smuggling in Sussex', *Sussex Archaeological Collection*, Vol X.

A Gentleman of Chichester. *A Full & Genuine History of the Inhuman & Unparalleled Murders of Mr William Galley & Mr Daniel Chater by Fourteen Notorious Smugglers* (pamphlet dated 1752).

'Jack Nastyface'. *Nautical Economy or Forecastle Recollections of Events in the Last War* (1835).

James, G. P. R. *The Smuggler*, a novel (1856).

Keble-Chatterton, E. *King's Cutters and Smugglers* (1908).

Marryat, Captain. *Two Cutters*, a novel (1841).

Russell Oakley, E. *The Smugglers of Christchurch, Bourne Heath & the New Forest* (1943).

Shore, H. N. *Smuggling Days and Smuggling Ways* (1892).

Shore, H. N. *Old Foye Days* (1907).

Bibliography

MANUSCRIPT SOURCES

Board of Customs Letter Books: ports of Hull, Ipswich and Rochester, 1725–56.
Instructions to Coastguard, 1832 and 1866.
Ministry of Defence (Navy) Library:
  Rear-Admiral HRH The Duke of Edinburgh: reports, 1879–92.
  An untitled collation of papers consisting of official reports of the taking of Russian prizes of war during April 1854 and subsequent correspondence.
  Shelburne Papers, Vol III.

RECOMMENDED FURTHER READING

Browning, H. J. *They Didn't Declare It* (1967).
Carson, E. *The Ancient and Rightful Customs* (1972).
Farjeon, J. Jefferson. *The Compleat Smuggler* (1938).
Halliday, F. E. *A History of Cornwall* (1959).
Harper, Charles G. *Smugglers* (1909; repr Newcastle 1966).
Verrill, A. H. *Smugglers and Smuggling* (1924).
Warneford, Lieut R. *Tales of the Coastguard* (1856).

Author's Note and Acknowledgements

I have, of necessity, taken pains to preserve the anonymity of my serving colleagues in the final chapter of this book. I am confident however that they will recognise themselves and will be recognised by others in the Customs service.

This book has not, of course, any official status and HM Commissioners of Customs and Excise accept no responsibility for its content.

My thanks are due to the following for their kind interest and assistance to me in my self-imposed task: Edward Carson, Librarian, and his staff of the Customs Library; Maurice Nockles and George Binks of the Customs Press Office; the staff of the Ministry of Defence (Navy) Library at Fulham; R. Allan Broadbent, editor of *Portcullis*, the Customs departmental magazine, and Michael Dodd, assistant editor, to whom I am indebted for most of the illustrations; Cdr H. S. May, RN (retd), late Deputy Chief Inspector of Coastguards; Mary Spriggs, who typed the manuscript and uncomplainingly produced order out of chaos; and finally to all those colleagues of high and lowly rank who, decently hiding their incredulity, came forward to offer their own invaluable contributions.

Authors Note and Acknowledgements

I have drawn upon a number of published sources including H. N. Shore's *Smuggling Days and Smuggling Ways* and E. Keble-Chatterton's *King's Cutters and Smugglers*. To D. Arnold-Forster, author of *At War with the Smugglers* I am indebted for documentary material quoted on pages 38–40, 50, 57–8.

My thanks are also due to Mr Henry Baynham, author of *From the Lower Deck* (Hutchinson 1969), and to his publishers for permission to quote from the journal of Samuel Stokes.

The illustrations are reproduced by courtesy of the following:

Mr P. Andrews, MBE, pages 42 (upper), 121

Mr F. C. Crossman, page 27.

Department of Trade and Industry and HMSO, page 142.

HM Commissioners of Customs and Excise, pages 18, 20, 29, 30, 53 (calligraphy by Mr B. V. Collins), 58, 79, 83, 92, 99, 105, 109, 111, 125, 129.

HM Stationery Office, pages 35, 37, 42 (lower), 74, 133, 137, 144, 145.

National Maritime Museum, London, 55, 102.

Miss Claire Phillipson, pages 61, 70.

Index

Page numbers in italic indicate illustrations

Aldington Gang, 85, 96–7
Argus, Revenue cutter, 109, 123, 124, *125*
Arnold, William, Collector of Customs, 35–6, 38–9

Benbechula, HMS, 128, *129*
Bonaparte, 88
Bow Street runners, 95–6
Browning, David ('Smoker'), 55–6
Burns, Robert, *29*, *30*, 31

Carter, Captain Henry, 93
Cawsand, smugglers, 89, 90, 91
Chater, Daniel, 80–2, *83*
Coast blockade, 94–6, 99, 103
Coastguard, 100–10, 126
Coast Preventive Service, 110
Comben, Richard, cutter commander, 43

Compensation payments, 43
Concealments of contraband, 61–2, 64, 68–72, 131–2, 142–4
Contraband cargoes, and fiscal policies, 16
Contract system, 32–5, 101
Coopers, 68, 109
Courtenay, Sir William, 67–8
Crimean War, 122–6
'Crop-sowing', *61*, 61–3, 64, 86
Customs Consolidation Order, 1822, 101
Customs Investigation Branch, 132, 135, 139; Launch Service, 129
Cutters *see* Revenue cutters

Dawn Approach, 131–3, 135
Deal, coup at, 26
Drug smuggling, 141–4

Index

Duke of Edinburgh, Rear Admiral, 106

Eagle, Revenue cutter, 55, 66
East Indiamen, 68–9

Fildon I, 139–41
Florida HMS, 116–17

Galley, William, 80–2, *83*, 85
Goudhurst, attack upon, 82, 84
Greyhound, Revenue cutter, 55, 101, 122
Guernsey, and smuggling, 86–8

Hawk, Revenue cutter, 52
Hawkhurst Gang, 79–82, 84–5
Henderson, Admiral Sir Reginald, 108
Hinde, Revenue cruiser, 114–15
Holland, Lord, 13

Immigrants, illegal, 15, 112
Import Duties Act, 1932, 110
Impressment, exemption from, 44
Industrial Revolution, effect on smuggling, 105
Investigation Branch, 132–3, 134, 135, 140, 141

'Jack Nastyface', 47–8
Juries, perverse verdicts of, 28, 54, 65

Kent, smuggling in, 77–85
Kingsmill, Thomas, 79–80, 84–5
Kite, HMS cutter, 56

Landguard, 100
Lark, Revenue cutter, 52, 54

Letters of marque, 118, 119

Mariner, 'deputed', 41
Marryat, Captain, 48
McCulloch, Captain J. M., RN, 95–6
Methodism, in Cornwall, 92
Mitchell, Captain, 55, 56

Newman, Richard, Riding Officer, 73
Nimble, Revenue cutter, 101
North Kent Gang, 85, 95–6

Orestes, HMS, 36
'Owlers', 16, 77, 82

Palmer, Henry, smuggler, 64
Pellew, Admiral Sir Edward (Lord Exmouth), 52, 54
Pellew, Samuel, Collector of Customs, 52, 54
Pensions, 43
Pioneer, HMS, 115
Pitt, William, 26
Poole Custom House, raided, 80
Potter, Thomas, smuggler of Polperro, 114
Preventive boats, 63–4, 97–9
Preventive Waterguard *see* Waterguard
Privateers, 40–1, 118, 120
Prize money, 118–19, 122, 124–5
Protection, Customs, 44

Revenue cutters, 32–49, 113–26, 135–9
crews of, 41, 43–6, 56–7, 100–1, 108, 137–8
general description, 36–7, 48
in 1909, 108

in inter-war period, 112, 128
in post-war period, 128
see also List of Illustrations, 9, 10
Rewards for seizures, 31
Roscoff (Rusco), 88, 90–1, 93
Royal Navy, relations with Customs, 46–8
Ruthven, George, Bow Street runner, 96–7

Sarmon, Francis, Captain, 41, 119–20
Shelburne, Lord, Home Secretary, 51
Shore, H. N. (Lord Teignmouth), 21, 24, 62–3, 89–91
Shorncliffe, 96
Signalling, illegal, 73–4
Smith, Sydney, 17
Smuggling Bill, 1736, 19, 28
Stephenson, William, smuggler, 115–16
Stokes, Samuel, mariner, 44, 56–7
Swallow, Revenue cutter, 55, 56
Swan, Revenue cutter,
   I 35–6
   II 36
   III 119–20, *121*

IV 41, 120
V 41, 43

Taku, 133–5

Uniforms, 49

Valiant, HMRC, *42*, 130, 135–6
Venturous, HMRC, 136–7, *137*, 140–1
Vigilant, HMRC, 69, *109*, *111*, 128–30, 137
Vincent, HMRC, 130, 135–6

Walcheren expedition, 118
Warneford, Lieutenant R., RN, 12
Waterguard,
   establishment of, 97–8
   consolidation with Coastguard, 100–1
   post-war, *74*, 129, 130, *133*, 137–9, 143
Wellard, smuggler, 52, 54
Wesley, John, 92
Westcountry smugglers, 85–93
Whitehead, Captain, 55
Women smugglers, 25

6 121